ROCKER BYE BABY

Claire Mear

A CIP catalogue record for this book is available from the British Library.

ISBN 978-1-9989922-0-1

Book layout and design by Clare Brayshaw

Front cover original artwork Meya Carlström Age 11 from Sweden

All sub headings written by Brian Mear

Prepared and printed by:

York Publishing Services Ltd
64 Hallfield Road
Layerthorpe
York YO31 7ZQ

Tel: 01904 431213

Website: www.yps-publishing.co.uk

REVIEWS

Rocker Bye Baby engagingly weaves together mysticism, emotional intelligence, and hardcore reality. Claire Mear is a sassy guide through her own journey, from a rough childhood, through to fertility issues, the tragic loss of a baby, and, finally, a hard-won happy ending. Mear busts through comfort zones, takes life by the horns, leans into her own rawness,' and shows us how our deepest vulnerabilities can lead to our greatest superpowers.'

Diana Rico (DianaRico.com)

'This is a beautifully written biography; you won't just read it but walk Claire's journey alongside her. You will not want to put it down. Young Claire had a lot to say, but no one wanted to listen. As a teenager she was placed in the care of social services, which awakened her realisation that the world was for her creative taking. Not letting her childhood define her, Claire went on to style the stars and was responsible for a few iconic outfits and looks of that time. She travelled extensively, became a Guatemalan Priestess, then helped countless people by becoming a London ambulance medic, moving into being a feature film medic. But she did not skip joyously through adult life. The hurdles got higher and potholes bigger. Enduring unimaginable pain, miscarriage, a full-term stillbirth, and depression. This did not stop Claire's creative drive. This book is proof that anyone can achieve anything, good can come from bad, no matter what our start in life. The phoenix always rises from the fire.'

Amelia Grimmett (creativemillie)

SILENT WHISPERS

Together, let us listen to the silent whispers of our lost children, as they collectively play within the Parklands of Shangri-La. Holding our broken hearts close, they guide us through the obstacles of our lament.

This book is for them and their brave parents and families.

Astrid & Charlie – 1983
Mathilde B – 14th October 1994
Rose & Petal – June 1996
Sunny & Angel Barrett – 30th October 1997
Eleesha Margaret Moore – 9th February 2006
Harrison Chapman – 8th April 2007
Tayte Souter-Symes – 13th February 2009
Robin Aniolkowski-Green – 25th February 2010
Baby Prokopenko-Rose – 24th May 2012.
Molly Mear – 12th August 2013
Baby Zeniou – 20th May 2015
Adora Elsie Klann – 11th September 2015
Bertie Roux Kent-Sweetman – 8th December 2015
Orion-Ten Cosmic Mear – 18th October 2016
Little Star De Almeida – September 2017
Malakai Le Grange – 12th June 2018
Grace Eleanor Seppman – 30th May 2019
Gracie Hudson – 30th May 2020

I wish to extend this dedication.
To all the children guiding us from the Heavens,
for which there are too many to name.

ABOUT THE AUTHOR

Claire Mear is a 53-year-old Aquarian dreamer. This is her first publication. Claire, along with her husband Brian, created a metal music festival called *Mearfest* in memory of their still-born daughter Molly. Alongside this genre of music, it brings to the fore awareness of miscarriage, stillbirth, and Down syndrome issues. Her life's mantra is to ask for miracles, and never give up! She lives in Cromer, Norfolk.

Her life has been based on a true story.

GRATITUDE IS MY TREASURE

I feel blessed with abounding gratitude and grace to all the people directly connected to this, my story. The first accolade goes to my husband Brian, for being right by my side throughout the most desperate times in later life. When blinded by the obvious, he became my eyes, when silence deafened, he was my ears. When mind, body, and spirit were fractured, crushed, and broken, he was my splint. He held my hand, keeping us moving forward right through the eye of every storm.

Brian Mear, I LOVE YOU.

Diana Rico, known as 'The Midwife of Authors,' a fitting title for this venture. Her long-term belief in me, along with her expertise in this field was consciously digested during its preliminary conception. I followed her sound advice to the letter, which pulled me though into its first trimester of creation.

Linnet Kerr has been my North Star. Her honesty, transparency, and good humour, seamlessly blended with her enthusiasm, has pulled me through some arcane times. Her direct involvement with my spiritual evolution, along with my novice wordsmithery, has seen this book flourish almost painlessly into its second and third-trimester stages.

During the trickiest latter stages of third-trimester fruition, Gabriole Springford leapt to the challenge. Her unique forward vision, subtle editing wisdom, along with her no-nonsense approach in getting this job done, have with no doubt, guided me through many frustrating weeks of heartburn, headaches, and due date hiccups. She has become my literary Doula by helping birth these pages from my laptop into the world.

Thank you to Duncan Beal and Clare Brayshaw from York Publishing House, for their confidence in me, expert advice and help in all things publishing.

My deepest heartfelt gratitude to the following: Tracey Smith, for decoding squiggly writing on official reports and being my soundboard of forgotten childhood memories. Joanne, Karen, and Tony Cawthorn for taking me in. To Richard and Sarah Bolland for keeping me in your hearts. Neville Hull for getting me through school and for sticking around some forty years later. Bailey, thank you for keeping me safe as a vulnerable child. Kim Bowen for believing in me in the workplace. Michael Newling, my listener, my believer, my lifetime confidant. Brenda Rivett, forever holding me close and keeping your word on Earth and from Heaven. Gratitude to Marina Banks, Chaplain Steve Sankley, Alva and Ella Chapman, Claire D'Breo, Catherine Morris, Vincent Fuller and Dr Charles, Paula Da Luz, Penny Abatzi, Jo Clairvoyant, Jacqui Deevoy and To Keep Watch. Love to Angela Holland, The Rev Carl Flynn, Anthony Bray, Amelia Grimmett and Elly Carter for being test readers.

To all our Mearfest supporters, from the benevolence of my heart, I thank you.

Molly, my soul yearns for you. Your crazy spirit has kept my dimmed inner light flickering through the darkest of midnight hours. My promises have been honoured to you and the Heavens. My first-born lives on within all of us who believe.

Finally, thank you to my little Doodie, who at the eleventh-hour restored love into my shattered heart, ushering me back from the brink of defeat. This book is for both my girls, mummy loves you last life, this life and into our next lives and beyond.

'*MY REALITY IS YOUR FICTION*'

IN MY NAME

I had no voice
So, talk for me
I could not move
So, walk for me
I could not smile
So, shine for me
I could not hold
So, touch for me
I could not hear
So, sing for me
I could not write
Say words for me
Born in the dark
So, see for me
No beating heart
So, love for me.

By Brian Mear

ONE

The End.

"Your baby's heart has stopped; I am so sorry, but your baby is dead." The monitor had been tilted away from view. We were unable to hear the familiar beeping, whooshing, galloping sounds that we had looked forward to since the twelve-week scan, twenty-seven weeks ago. To us, this was a whole lifetime. The senior consultant midwife had just started her weekend call, she took a deep breath in, composed herself further, solemnly turning her head in my direction. Softly, she repeated for a second time those four devastating words, just in case I did not hear them correctly the first time, "Your baby is dead." I did not want to hear them, how could our precious baby, the one we had already named Molly be dead?

Five litres of haemoglobin, suddenly caramelised under trembling epithelium. The consultant studied the ultrasound, her lips became bunched, causing a deep frown line that was vertical from her widow's peak to the top of her threaded brow. Her head and shoulders hung low, knowing she was the bringer of devastating news. Nothing but bleak dismal words were coming from her mouth. Everything from this point onwards was about to change. The doctor's experienced eyes held their gaze on the small monochrome screen. As she gently tapped the top corner of the monitor with her left index finger, her unwavering right hand guided the foetal doppler, which skated in every direction above my precious unborn child. Fear clogged every vein. I had failed at being a mother at the last hurdle, leaving me utterly bereft. My right ear suddenly developed a series of deafening frequency changes, and my auditory canal was under attack. The sudden onset of pain tore right through me, piercing, then paralysing, listening to those same spoken words of death that it refused to hear.

This type of demise is called an intrauterine foetal death, a terminology I had never heard of before this day. Even though I am medically trained and had been working for various ambulance services over the last two decades, no one is ever prepared for, or ever imagines, that this will happen to them. Molly had made it to her thirty-ninth week of life before death. She was technically a full-term baby; her due date was in two days, growing to her 69th centile for her gestational age. Molly could not have been more perfect, her induction was booked for Monday, the day after tomorrow, the nursery was ready with life-sized wild animal wall stickers, and enough nappies to last until she is eighteen. My job was to be her mummy, her bosom, her maternal guide in life, and Brian, her daddy, her provider, her support system.

The consultant, along with a very silent, almost terrified, young trainee midwife, shuffled out of the room together. I did not cry, because every blood cell within my marrow instantly dried up. Brian tried to control his emotions to be strong for me, but a dam buster came out of nowhere, crumbling his tough, Leo sun-sign exterior, successfully bombing a hole right through his heaving chest. Brian's tears fell in natural grieving torrents, drowning out his dreams of ever having a daughter. His broken-hearted body swooped down to my left side, to give me a comforting hug, but I lay in complete shock on the hospital bed. There was no weeping, just an instant refusal to believe this cruel trick of nature was happening to us. The English doctor stood by me on the right side of the bed, just to make sure I could understand this bit of the negotiations. She tried to explain in over-pronounced English, as if I was a foreigner living within my own country, that they do have a protocol in place for this kind of situation.

"Claire, we will give you one pill, this will hopefully reverse time by forty-eight hours." Within my mind I felt like Mrs Hindsight, as she would have rung the labour ward two days ago when her instincts were on red alert. My mind nattered on and on. I remembered that one moment when I felt a bit funny but decided not to mention this to anyone, so as not to cause any fuss. "You would have been placed on the monitors and Molly would have been born alive sometime on Monday, or possibly Tuesday, as planned in your original birthing notes." Surely this cannot be happening to us! "Claire, we will give you one pill to start the labour process. You must go home now, there is nothing more we can do for you today. Please come back on Monday morning at eight o'clock as planned, and we will assist induction if nothing has happened by then." Screaming out, I asked, "Is that it?" As though the more dramatic part of this script had been axed, due to a lack of funding. "Yes, that is it. I am truly very sorry for your loss," the doctor said as she looked me squarely in the eyes. "But why can't you C-section me now?" I asked, with a tone of utter desperation coming from inside a strangled voice box. The doctor came closer and took my hand in hers. "My dear, in time, this will all make sense; it is a tried and tested part of the natural grieving process. We have done these hundreds of times before, trust me." As if I trusted anything right now!

"We do have a particular room for this kind of delivery; fortunately, you will be set back away from this unit." How fortunate to be hidden away, banished to a secret room like in the darker days of history. The clock on the wall said a quarter past Saturday afternoon, as I nervously swallowed the little pill, which sat alone within a miniature paper cup. I had questions. Did she die two days ago when I felt incredibly tired and could hardly move due to the August heatwave? I remember she moved yesterday, Friday. I had a friend come around in the morning, she thrashed around then, we both saw and felt her life force under my stretched skin. We found this endearing, but maybe this was her in distress, trying to get out.

Unbearable physical cramping hit immediately, almost before we had made it out to the car park. The intense, crippling pain felt nothing like period pain, which was no doubt compounded by my shock. We were at the hospital less than an hour, in that short time we transitioned from, 'can you pee in this pot' to 'take this death pill,' then finally to 'see you in two days.' It was all so quick. Brian had hastily parked the car taking up one and a half spaces, as we were so panicked to get into the hospital on time, by this point, I had not felt her move for a few hours. Luckily, there was no parking ticket left on the window, someone must have told the security guy as this never happens in Royal Berkshire.

Once home, disbelief turned into atheism. What kind of God could do this to us? Anger rumbled in the air like thunder. Much rain was needed; it had been a long dry summer since early May, and all the plants in our patio garden had wilted. At this moment, nature was mirroring human life. Marina had been my dear friend for over twenty years, she was waiting for us at home. She is a practising life coach and zen mother to four independent creative children, and she was meant

4

to be Molly's godmother. Marina had received the call from Brian, and without hesitation had rushed up from Brighton to Oxfordshire to help with the early stages of induced labour. Staggering around the garden patio, at a loss of how to feel or what to do next, Marina wanted to keep me moving, and above all, calm. "Breathe, Clairey, breathe. Now, in through the nose, and out through the mouth, yes, very good." Ironically, it started spitting drops of rain, giving life back to the roots of the wilted greenery in the garden. "Hey, feel that Clairey, teardrops from Molly." It was the best Marina could do for her friend.

Brian sat bereft inside the open plan living room; glued to a sticky leather armchair, paralysed by fear, grief, and bewildered new emotions. He was dazzled under the unprotected glass sunroof, the intense glare made him sweat and squint through his tears even more. He was being comforted by his twenty-year-old son Adam, who was equally trying hard to get his head around the fact that his little sister was gone. As Molly's father, Brian was as lost, helpless, and as beyond words as I was, minus the constantly swollen ankles, painfully cramped right hamstring, a rotting wisdom tooth, and a pyro-infused oesophagus.

Before today, all maternal aches and pains had been dealt with by using natural remedies, just in case anything more substantial harmed our miracle, baby girl. Around tea time, the labour pains became a little harder to tolerate. This was a new kind of intense pain; one I had never anticipated would feel so spiteful. Awkwardly pacing a figure of eight between the outside and inside space, Marina guided my breathing, as I carried Molly's due weight to the end. Our umbilical connection was intact, she was still very much a part of me. Occasionally, excitement surfaced as tiny flutters gave the illusion she had awoken. The truth was evident; this earthly chrysalis had broken free, our eidolon butterfly fluttered away, further upward to be closer to her true creator. Her lifeless vessel suspended in amniotic fluid, gently knocking against the pier of her wrecked mother's uterus. Cheekily I prayed for a second miracle, asking the Gods if they would not mind waking her up. Noting that if this was a joke, it had gone on long enough.

By Sunday morning, everyone had left us alone, and the earlier labour pains had all but stopped; there was nothing but stillness. I had waited decades for this very moment of procreation. This pregnancy had not been planned as such because I was forty-six years old. We had given up all hope, especially since being told a couple of years earlier, by the finest fertility experts in London, that my womb had evidence of decay, that clogged its way up through my fallopian tubes and beyond. It was as if 'do not enter' red tape had been hastily wrapped all around my reproductive organs, that now resembled a crime scene. Regardless of this, the previous December, a little voice in my head said, "take a test." The in-date digital stick proudly announced I had been a mother for three whole weeks; this was nothing short of a modern-day miracle.

We hatched a plan to reduce my working week, as I bounced between being a frontline and feature film ambulance medic. I hurtled myself into each new maternity obstruction like a suffragette. As Molly took shape and grew to her perfect centile, not one prescription drug passed my lips. At twenty weeks, we were told by a Harley Street doctor that she had Down syndrome. The unique Harmony blood test confirmed she was 99% positive for T21, why us?

We were in meltdown for a couple of weeks, until it dawned on us that this baby had chosen us for her journey. Still, mixed messages were coming our way. The consultants at the hospital did not believe she had Down syndrome; she had no positive markers and all the scans stated that there must be a problem with the Harmony test, as there were no prominent abnormal appearances. Whether she had Downs or not, she was our daughter, we had between us created her physical body. We were going to keep her.

I constantly sought healing assistance through new age remedies; reiki, angelic whispering, acupuncture, reflexology, Zen this and universal that. I even had my auric field photographed at thirty weeks, which was rich in healing blues and vibrant purples. Everything positive had been thought about and researched, all-natural wholesome and holistic practices utilised to ensure she would arrive safely, but I still felt that I had somehow failed her. My mind fabricated possibilities; in a past life, I must have been a hated politician, maybe a monstrous serial killer, or an evil dictator to deserve this kind of birth-right karma.

The day before Molly was to be induced, a twisting vine of darkness grabbed at both ankles, dragging me into a coffin of dejection. My thoughts became jumbled, like fragmented lost data. An overpowering hatred of myself aggressively plucked at struggling vocal cords. I thought that I had enough conviction to be a good mother, but my body had already failed her before I got the chance. The Western Gods to whom I had prayed to quite a lot lately for her safe delivery, were obviously not real. I felt conned and cheated by everything and everyone. Over the last few months of gestation, this little life had helped me to accept a new mature role of responsibility. It had been a privilege and an honour to carry her. Images flooded my mind of not being alive after tomorrow, thoughts of dying entertained my soul-searching mind, what other options were there? Brian and I would undoubtedly split up; as we dealt with the desperation, confusion, loss, and guilt in our own separate ways. We had both suffered enough. We were two different people sharing the same disaster; this was surely cancer in the making.

Monday morning arrived, induction day. Before we set off, I bathed in luxuriously scented bubbles, gifted to me at her baby shower, intended to help me relax after she was born alive. The summer sunlight danced through waving trees from the garden, so that shadows bounced around the privacy window, hitting my inert bump like a flickering spotlight in a ghost town. I held my tummy, said goodbye aloud, my tears disguised by the humidity of the bathwater. On this dark day of induction, I wore a new floral printed dress, that weeks ago I had bought two clothing sizes too big, perfect for now, reaching a full forty weeks into gestation. Finally, we had arrived at her due date, but sadly she had already been dead for more than forty-eight hours. Today, Molly would be born sleeping, beneath the black twill of printed cotton flowers.

Room eleven is a special place for couples like us to give birth to death. The room was indeed conveniently tucked away from all the happy, healthy, alive, screaming babies. It was also far from their excited weary parents, extended families, and loyal friends, joyously supporting them through the unbearable physical suffering that is parturition. Medical instructions did not sink into my foggy head during this kind of personal, yet awkward situation. I had pressing questions, like why I had to carry her for two whole days? I knew if a baby went without oxygen for that long, it would not be looking good upon delivery. A natural vaginal delivery was part of my original birthing plan, but so was a healthy breathing baby. No one ever discussed plan B. Now we were part of the hospital's well-rehearsed stillbirth protocol, bringing me more indescribable physical pain on top of mounting emotional ravages.

Delivering my bundle of doom in private, she was never going to be a somebody, no life to hold within empty arms. There would be no family with us to share our joy; my best girlfriends found it too hard even to think Molly dead, let alone be with us in the hidden away delivery suite. No one kept us updated on social media gossip, as I believed without a doubt that I would be the next online subject of idle chit chat. What kind of a medically trained Kali Goddess am I, who cannot bring my dead daughter back to life?

Room eleven had every detail carefully examined by the midwives running the maternity ward, and those on the Willow support group committee. They had all, in some way and at some point, travelled through this same bleak tunnel of hopelessness. The bookshelf held carefully chosen literature, highlighting the specialist subjects of death and grieving, with an assortment of sweet poems illustrated in pastel watercolours. Hundreds of prudently constructed words of comfort, understanding, and positive outcomes that had come from experienced broken-hearted parents, were printed in mollifying Garamond, ready to guide us, the newly bereaved, to accept our fate. We were room eleven's next victims. As much as these books piqued my curiosity, I could not look at sweet illustrations, or read words of support in any languages, printed or even on a brightly lit HD screen. This was the only time in my whole life when I screamed out silently, in the most colourful language of all, RAGE.

Downloaded playlists had been collected then saved onto MP3, ranging from eighties pop, regressing back to seventies punk rock, all in pain threshold order, to get me through the processes of a natural delivery with a living baby. Now, I had no will to listen to any genre of music. Nor could I execute my well-rehearsed hypno-breathing techniques, which cost a fortune to learn. Once my cervix started to widen, and the pelvic-splitting later stages of labour kicked in, there was no pretending to give birth just by mindfully breathing more deeply, as had been practised in a rural village hall. My evolving faith in and appreciation of everything esoteric, holistic, and spiritual had ceased, when those four words, 'your baby is dead' had finally sunk in.

Noise did not sit well between my ears, even the muffled sounds of my heavy breathing hurt, as I sucked hard on the free-flowing Entonox. My voice became distinctively Pinky, if not a tad Perky. Going through this kind of labour, had to be the most painful experience of my entire life. Five hours in, my cervix had dilated by two centimetres, the midwife was a trainee, she kept submerging her whole arm up Molly's exit tunnel, just to check progress. I lost track of time. Several hours later, our young midwife's voice wafted into my inner ears that still sounded like an old transistor radio tuning in. I knew the stress of being a newly childless mother had given me tinnitus.

"Claire, can you hear me? You are ready." To her, this was still a birth, a stillbirth no less, something on the midwifery curriculum that every student dreaded. "Ready, for what?" I squeaked, my voice becoming more Perky than Pinky. "You are at ten centimetres; we need to prepare you to start pushing." It was still daylight, the time on the wall said a hazy seven something on a summer's evening, it was still Monday, the 12th night of August 2013. I needed Molly's life force more than ever, right this minute! I needed her to wriggle through this birth canal, with one hundred per cent determination to be born, to come from her heavenly world of harps and angels. It takes two forces of life to birth one baby, but she had no life left, it was all down to me now.

During that final hour, I was nothing short of maniacal, not knowing what to expect or how she would look. What would I feel when I saw my first-born, blackened, bruised, and forever sleeping? I was past caring as I pushed so hard my ears finally popped. I was seconds away from being Molly's mother, at least until the time of her cremation. The room filled with doctors and surgeons, desperately trying to get her out. The doctors multiplied, I could hear them coming and going, shouting instructions to each other, "The only way to get her out is to break the baby's shoulder." After another aggressive inhalation of gas and air, genuinely feeling confusion, I drifted off, somewhere above the indescribable pain, moments away from achieving an out-of-body experience.

TWO

They are the ones, that bind the truth
The oath is set, with concrete proof.

A sense of weightlessness ushered pieces of broken Claire over and beyond an arc of primary hues of mist and matter, free from fear or trauma and unaware of the enormity of what had just happened. Everything Earthly dissolved, nothing much felt relevant anymore, until out of this nothingness I heard a voice.

"Dearest Claire, you are safe, please do not be afraid." I felt far from afraid, I was intrigued, elated even. Was I dead? "We are your seven generations of Great-Grandmother Elders, and we wish to explain what is to happen next if you desire to continue this journey's path as Claire. We have brought you here today to ask you to make a tough, once in a few lifetime's decision. You will either give up your life as Claire and leave the planet right now or continue onwards as Claire and help your fellow people in this time of deepening global crisis and Aquarian transition." This sounded too good to be true, I was ready to die! But then there was the 'helping my fellow people' part, this was sounding complicated.

Hold on a second, I knew this voice; it was my maternal Grandma Anna, who spoke in a broken Austrian accent. Brian's mother, Sally, then introduced herself, as I had not met her since she had passed away just months before

Brian and I had met in 2010. Sally held my ethereal hand, as I soon realised, I did not have a physical hand.

A gloomy Victorian lady stood before me; her name was Aunt Ada. She wore a long, black, embroidered crinoline dress with a hooping bustle underneath; that I knew Vivienne Westwood would have been inspired by. She was a distant auntie on my father's side, I had no idea about her, as my entire family on both sides were consistently distant. Aunt Ada held what looked to be a new baby in her arms. At first, I thought it was Molly, but that thought dissolved into atom-sized grey particles, as this was not true. You cannot lie here, where ever 'here' is, not even little white lies, as they just blow up right in front of you.

Aunt Ada last lived around the 1870's and had lost her baby full-term in childbirth, just like I was doing right now. She yearned to be with her baby so much that she died days after childbirth, from complications of a broken heart. Eternity had held her first-and-only born till the now. A vision was projected into my minds' eye that I had taken on my ancestor's maternal trauma, it had been passed down to me for a reason. Somehow, I was to complete our unfinished DNA family business and free my auntie's soul, and her baby, forever.

My beloved Brenda appeared, she looked around the age I am now, mid-forties, even though she was eighty when she passed just the year before. Brenda was my mother's best friend from the age of sixteen, when they both worked at London's Peter Jones' shoe department, back in the early sixties. Brenda was the only person who stood by me while growing up, and then on into adulthood. The minute we saw each other again, she was beyond any sensible human words. Brenda's face beamed utter happiness, she looked good, death really suited her. Brenda thanked Brian and me for walking her through her final stages of cancer, hospice, and death. She commented that she was so amused and grateful when I decorated the exterior of her Eco-cardboard coffin, with photos, drawings, and random letters to and from the City Council, as she loved to bring community issues to their attention. Brenda explained that it was a painless and rather enjoyable journey into the afterlife.

A clear image of a five-year-old girl with thick, curly, dark auburn hair, cut into a sharp Sassoon-looking bob, now stood before me. This little girl wore the most out of this world dress. My heart instantly pounded four decades of misplaced maternal love beats. This was my unborn daughter Molly, but here in the world of spirit, she was five. Grandma Anna introduced us, during that second it dawned on me how much I had missed these people. I felt pained that I had never been able to get to know any of them well when they were alive, all thanks to my parents' insular worlds.

"Claire, we have suspended your life for a while, as we need to have a talk with you." This was serious, but then I realised everyone could hear my thoughts. Grandma Anna whispered in a more English than Austrian accent, so as not to bring up any traumatic triggers to do with my own, somewhat absent European mother. This was thoughtful of her, as I was going through quite enough right now. Grandma Anna also looked much younger than I last remembered.

"Suspended! Am I dead?" I had worked for the ambulance service, and I knew 'suspended' in medical terms usually meant quite dead. However, one might have had a chance of survival if someone jived on their sternum, to the Bee Gees soundtrack of *Staying Alive*, while delivering a shock of 360 joules into them by using a 12-lead ECG. "Well, sort of, you are delivering the vessel of Molly as we speak, but things have gone a little wrong. However, this was all planned many moon phases ago, so that we could have this opportunity to ask you, in person, how you wish to proceed?" My mind went blank, my brain could not take this all in, so for once I just listened.

"If you do wish to carry on with your life's contract, then we can arrange that, right now. You will be given specific instructions on what you will do with this situation for the most favourable outcome. We will send you back into your body of Claire, aged forty-six and six months; however, your daughter will still be born sleeping, as planned. Regarding meeting us, your guardians, seven generations of grandmothers and matriarchal loved ones, this will be disguised as a vivid dream or a déjà vu." I must have been mid-transit during an almighty out- of- body experience, this was too damn cosmic to be true.

Sally Mear continued. "Or, my love, if you do not wish to proceed, we can arrange for a medical complication to occur in the delivery room. This happens all the time. Your Aunt Ada, who is here with her baby today, had this same choice, but she was too afraid, angry, and broken to continue to see this through. Her timeline was not as global as yours is now, so you have a greater chance to succeed. If you agree to return, this will break Ada's endless cycle of grief, and both she and her baby will be set free. If you stay, you will not feel a thing. Your spirit is already here with us, there will simply be a slight snapping, like an elastic band at the top of your head. This is the silver cord that is your lifeline breaking away from your body, and this is when you pass over. The choice is entirely up to you."

"Well, how long do I have to decide?" I enquired, as I felt confused. I thought this kind of life or death decision was a God-thing, and not up to us. It appeared that time in the Heavens is a tricky subject to explain to a nearly dead human, who has few mortal seconds left to decide. "Can I speak with Molly?" It was previously revealed that her human body was just a vessel, which was never intended to travel to its destination. The bereavement/ handling guides had been called in a long time before I got pregnant. They felt it in our best interest to give Molly a challenging human physical condition, so they gave her Down syndrome. That was believed to be an avenue for grieving parents like Brian and myself to find some sort of solace, to help us cope with the loss a little better, maybe leading us into some form of related charity work.

For a few seconds, I absorbed the essence of my spirit daughter Molly. "Molly, my darling child. I do not care about any physical disabilities you may or may not have had. We both would have loved you to pieces and cared for you, regardless." As I talked to her through thoughts, shards of my shattered heart were carefully slotted back together by sound waves that looked like jigsaw pieces, glued solid by sticky energy. Molly transformed herself, shapeshifting into a colourful cloak of primary lights. Wrapping herself around my entire troubled spirit, every gentle colour surrounded my grief, which energised and aligned all my seven wonky flagging chakras.

"Mummy, how I love you both so much, I will always be your Molly. After today, will you allow my hand to guide you both? Your creativity and openness will help to achieve great things after this chapter turns to another page."

Since the age of fifteen, I never got to understand the emotions connected to genuine love, because my trust was smashed into pieces by those who brought me into this world back in 1967. But right this minute, pure love filled every inch of space between soul and flesh. Light and love were connecting all four broken human heart chambers, like a child's jigsaw. My physical body continued to lay motionless and unresponsive on the hospital bed surrounded by monitors and Brian, who was Molly's fraught father, and thankfully there were very smart doctors keeping everything in check. Molly continued, "Through my death, you will assist others in reaching their true potential, helping them understand their own losses, guiding them to find their dormant talents and lost confidences. I cannot begin to explain the enormous amount of work you and daddy have to do for this earth, commencing from today."

How is it that my baby is talking to me? She is so smart. "I will still be born, minutes from now, leaving a visible mark for you both and for the world. I promise to assist in your recovery by whispering instructions during quiet times. They will be perceived as night dreams and daytime intuitions, insights, and coincidences. You will hear my voice everywhere; it will be resting upon the hearts of all who believe. Your own broken heart will heal sooner than you think, as this process has already begun." How can this be true? I am dying of a broken heart right now and possibly postpartum haemorrhaging in that hospital bed; as my body had started bleeding out its old clotted life. I wanted to stay here with Molly forever. It is bliss having no physical body, no worries, no bills, no banks, no governments, no rules, nothing but my daughter and estranged family.

"We have special agents of spirit on Earth, to whom we have sent specific instructions, warning them that you will come knocking, looking for assistance. Even though I died, my spirit will be felt and seen, loud, proud, and colourful. My name, Molly Mear, will be spoken in many different languages. Goosebumps and tingling in your right hand will be my calling card." I imagined everyone present crying real tears, enough tears to hydrate all wilting plants in every global garden. "I need you to be stronger than ever before, I need you to get back into the body of Claire and see this challenge through. Open your giving heart. It will not break any further, it has been toughened over the years for this reason, but soon it will be fixed, and love will become you again. I am part of your spirit guide team from now forward. We had a soul agreement from many moon phases ago. Mummy, I was never meant to be born at this time." The love I felt for this little girl went beyond anything I had ever experienced or imagined before today.

Molly continued; I was transfixed by her eloquent comments. "You were meant to feel what it is like to carry your own child, to feel the unconditional love that, sadly, you never had from your mother. You need to feel the unbroken bond between mother and child. It is a beautiful, timeless, unconditional connection. Unfortunately, the bond from your mother to you was broken from the start, this will never be fixed. It is time to move on. Your mother's only purpose was to give birth to you and bring you to this planet; that is it, her job is now complete. I promise we all have much work to do to help all the people in need at this monumental time on Earth."

By this point, I knew I was somewhere in the Heavens. It had to be. If not, I had been given a massive dose of morphine and was on the trip of a lifetime. In that second, I could not think of any previous problems, including being newly childless, because here she was, talking to me and she was very much alive.

"Hold that thought, dear Claire." My spirit guide quickly stepped in; her name is To Keep Watch. She had to be the most feminine spirit I had ever seen, with an aura of female warrior strength, the magnitude of which took my breath away. Tall, slender, with exquisite facial features, I was in love. To Keep Watch continued, "Many women like you, dear Claire, are born warrior strong, and you have been guided to find your spiritual forte. Your Earthly experiences strengthened you until you became consciously alive, intuitive, creative, and observant. It has taken forty-six years to build you up to this day. Many other great females alive today, will also have special babies like Molly. These babies have a cardinal contract to complete. They will be born sleeping, in order to wake up their parents and everyone connected in seeing the world in its rawest, harshest forms. What could be more devastating than to hear that a baby has died? This opens the fearful hearts and closed minds of the faithless lost."

I was mesmerised, unable to avoid her hypnotic gaze. "Believe it or not, dear one, your whole life has been in training for what is to come. The seven great-grandmothers need you to turn this tragic event around and be warrior brave. This time in our history is global, and finally, digital miracles can be achieved with the click of a mouse. If you choose to complete this request, in recompense for the difficult, challenging and very public mission ahead, your angelic master team will promise to one day bring you much happiness and joy."

"I accept the challenge." Molly's death had bent, but not broken me. And so, with absolute faith, conviction, and determination to achieve this, my final goal, I returned into the body of Claire.

THREE

For the circle never ceases
That of mortality and death.

"Ok everyone, she's back, let's get this baby out!" A senior surgeon shouted to the room packed full of doctors, and officials with clipboards documenting every action taken. The beeping of faint monitors came back into my auditory arena. My blood pressure steadily climbed back up to normal levels. My heart rate alleviated the constant ebb and flow of life in the balance.

At that same moment over Stonehenge, just off the A360 at Airman's Corner, the annual Perseid meteor shower was lighting up the humid summer evening sky, enthralling captivated stargazers. In Berkshire on the Craven Road, darkness fell within room eleven, as I had successfully delivered my beautiful bundle of extinction. Molly, our own shining star, was born sleeping at 20:52 p.m, on the 12th night of August 2013.

"She has Down's, Claire, look at her eyes. I am going out for a walk back soon." With that, Brian left the room. The doctors respectfully cut the cord on his behalf. Wiggling my sore bottom up the bed, still wearing the black floral dress now soaked in amniotic fluids and blood, I sat up. Shrouded within a donated pink hand-knitted shawl, Molly's lifeless body was gently handed to me.

Both of my empty aching arms finally got to hold my longed-for daughter's bruised and silent body. No crying, no rise and fall of her fragile chest as her breath had already been stolen. Glimpses of her eyes made me feel helpless and sad, as both her lids slid open, exposing jet-black eyeballs, her fingernails and lips the same colour, all caused by the lack of oxygen and life. The explanation of why it was better to go through three days of torment by following the NHS natural birthing processes, was in part to do with the physical recovery. C-section stitches would limit mobility, and all that raw, maternal grief barricading itself in there, would escape when I least expected it. If I were to get pregnant again, even though at my current age of forty-six, that thought was nothing short of a joke, a secondary C-section would be out of the question. This was the more practical solution all round, but I would rather have been immobile for the rest of my sorry life if I could have held her sooner. Still, the two-day delay did give us precious time with Molly safe inside to try to come to terms with what was about to happen. Once she was out, the physical pain was quickly forgotten. Emotional pain instantly backed up within my arteries like cholesterol paintballing its way to obliterated chambers of my heart. Brian came back to the room and sat beside Molly and me.

"Brian," I whispered. "Now, this might sound strange, but I am sure I just met your mother, my Grandma Anna, Brenda, and guess what, Molly was there too. I saw Molly. She is alive and well and five years old, but she is just not physically here." Apart from the giving birth part, I felt that something almighty had happened. "Darling, you were in shock. Literally, you were unresponsive for a good few minutes. They even got the crash kit out. I could not do anything; I was helpless. I'm so sorry, I thought I was losing you." Brian had confirmed that I was unresponsive for a few minutes, yet wherever that place was, it felt like hours.

The midwives kept Molly in the present, saying that 'she is my beautiful daughter,' and after nine long months, finally, 'she is here in my arms.' They refrained from speaking of her as deceased, because she is in the here and in the now, just like an Eckhart Tolle quotation. She had that new baby feel, her body fragile and floppy, with soft rounded chubby cheeks, her blackened cupid lips drooped, due to reduced muscle tone. Laid outstretched, she had the longest post mortem stained legs, ten toes and fingers that were all the same length, which was unusual. The skin on her hands and feet had wrinkled and peeled away through dehydration.

After one last push, her wretched placenta arrived in dark red clumps, due to it not functioning over the previous three days or maybe more, as we did not know exactly when she died. The doctor gave me another pill, which would stop lactation, my breasts were now officially redundant. An older midwife suggested I bathe her with warm water, dabbing, not wiping her with cotton wool balls, as her damaged skin peeled like a burn's victim. Afterwards, we gently placed her into the smallest nappy I had ever seen.

Oddly, the number one single in the UK Independent charts on this Molly's birth-date was 'Let Her Go,' by Passenger. Dressing her in a baby-grow with 'BA/BY' written in ac/dc rock fonts, since Brian was a lifetime heavy metal devotee, I carefully wiggled the neckline over her partially crushed skull. Initially, this outfit was for our first baby pictures to parade proudly on Facebook, but there would be no public photos uploaded anywhere, I felt too ashamed. Our first private photos were of us both holding her, Brian could barely raise a smile. The feeling of pride was pushed down, hidden beneath the surface, and yet I had given birth in less than twelve hours, and our daughter was finally here. Mixed emotions prevailed, inside I was crying for our loss, but on the outside, I felt delighted to be holding her, while I forced a fake photo smile. Brian had watched me bathe her fragile body. He said he felt that I would have been a fantastic mother. This was music to my ears, and since this was the only time I would be a functioning mother making the most of every little thing I could do for her while she was still with us.

Molly had been wrapped up like a caterpillar in a cocoon, then placed in a cuddle cot. This was a relatively new invention to keep her core body at colder temperatures. Going against nature itself, I had to rest my newborn in a chest freezer. I stood to my feet unaided, as promised, I did indeed feel great, my post-birth uterus did not hurt in any way. There was no need for stitches, which was a miracle considering they broke her shoulder while she was still inside. All of this added up to high accolades for hospital stillbirth procedures.

I walked unaided into the En-suite shower, stretched both arms out in front of me and yawned as it was getting late in the evening. I held onto the green-tiled wall in front and pulled the floral dress off from my aching shoulders, it fell to the ceramic floor with a thud. Suddenly, an unexpected wrench tugged at my conscience. The dress had stayed on throughout the delivery, collecting our blood, that had ingrained itself into its very fabric. A moment of confusion surfaced, which waste bin do I use, general, recycling, or clinical? The clinical waste bin felt more appropriate, as it deserved its own cremation and order of service within the hospital's incinerators. Spiritually, our umbilical had not severed, Molly stood beside me as my disappointment was washed from my tired body, swirling clockwise down into the plughole beneath. Bashing the wall with my bare fists as I bit my inner lip till it bled, desperately wishing to primal scream into Kingdom come, I refrained from any vocal release at all. I did not want to traumatise Brian and the nurses any further.

Molly weighed a respectable 7 lbs and 9 oz. Both hips flexed, her right shoulder dropped where it had been broken, extremities blackened through lack of oxygen, with a drooping jaw like a stroke victim, but regardless I loved her; I loved every inch of this broken baby. The midwife managed to take a snippet of hair, and six instant polaroid photos. The flash of the camera captured every nuance, bringing her briefly back to life. Ink prints of Molly's hands and feet had been skillfully copied onto a thick cream textured card. All these pieces of memorabilia had been neatly placed within a keepsake booklet. It felt as if we had attended a forty-week seminar of how to make a baby, with craft activities included as part of the programme itinerary. There are no words to begin to describe the disappointment that this was everything that was left. This memory box became my own personal metaphoric aneurysm.

Midnight struck, ascending us into the following day of realisation that we still had nothing living to take home with us. The nurses did their final checks before we all went to sleep in the same donated double bed. Sadly, I was still alive, Molly was not, as she lay next to us both in her cuddle cot, that made the room glow a light blue and hummed all night like our kitchen fridge.

We heard no crying, whimpering, sucking noises, no night feeds, or vomit spewed onto my shoulders. There were no latching issues or sore nipples, nor were there lessons on how to wind correctly, from the night shift midwives. No nappy changes, or unanswered questions of things you do not think about before your first baby is born. I had been spared such tiresome worries. Molly looked peaceful as if she was asleep, this was the only time I felt part of the most beautiful family on Earth. I hardly slept, not wanting to miss a single minute of being with her, as I knew what was coming in the morning. As she lay peacefully next to us, her core body temperature continued to freeze. My redundant breasts throbbed, already in a battle between the draining milk duct medication and mother nature, both fighting each other like heroic mammary matadors. Still, no tears surfaced. My lifeless baby was here, right in front of me, stillborn from my Jurassic womb, which, just three years earlier, held no hope at all for the creation of human life. By degree, it still gave me this.

We were given as much time as we needed with her in room eleven. Since the next thirty years were out of the question so, we settled on fifteen hours and twenty-five minutes. Holding Molly close, I talked to her, believing she would respond, lovingly kissing her, breathing her in, stroking her bruised raw cheeks with my Shrek sized fingers. Eventually, she got too warm, then started to smell, so I had to return her to the cuddle cot. Brian felt it hard to hold her at all during this time. I found this odd, as he was a dad to his grown-up son. Alongside his time as a father, he had been a paramedic for twenty-five years, experiencing many traumatic situations far worse than this, but this was his baby, his longed-for daughter, his trauma. Many times, Brian made excuses to leave the room, experiencing another kind of father-crushing sadness on the outside of our protected room eleven bubble. Once stepping into the corridors beyond, he was faced with other dads rushing around, not really knowing what was going on, holding lists of instructions from exhausted new mums, carrying complicated car seats, and bulging nappy bags stuffed with every eventuality. Visiting friends and relatives hung on to helium balloons with 'it's a boy,' or 'it's a girl,' printed on gender correct foil, while some parents were lucky enough to have twins. Brian's only solace was inside room eleven.

The following morning, I laid across a two-seater sofa, holding my beautiful seraph tight with my long bare legs hanging over the arms, when the midwife knocked on the door. As she entered, I did not bother to move, it was too comfortable holding my first and only child in my arms, feeling like a mother doing my duties. Speaking respectfully in hushed tones, the midwife spoke directly to my legs. "Claire, I need to tell you that we have a hospital Chaplain, you should maybe think about having Molly blessed and named by him." Had she not realised that my previous belief in God and whatever faith I had left in spirit had dissolved three days ago? "I do not believe in any God; what God kills babies? So, no thank you very much." I was adamant. She continued. "I appreciate you're deeply upset, but maybe talk it through with Brian when he returns, he might want to see the Chaplain himself."

Brian returned a little after, I told him what had happened. "Claire, this would be the most perfect thing to do right now, seriously what about what I want?" Brian was trying his best to conceal his disappointment in everything. "But there is no frigging GOD, she's dead!" Trying to control my adult hurting, feeling like a child about to throw myself onto the floor, my face screamed at him through puffy damp rouge cheeks, as neither of us were anywhere near the eye of this storm quite yet. "But I need the Chaplain guy! What about what I need, I lost her too, remember. I thought I was going to lose both of you. You were gone, gone Claire, and I could not do a thing about it." Brian was visibly cracking.

That same day, on the 13th of August 2013, the Netherlands' famous windmills had all stopped turning, they were stationary, stuck in the traditional mourning position to mark the death of Prince Johan Friso. Gigantic sinkholes appeared in parts of Florida, swallowing up whole homes, all reflective of my own feelings. If only a big sinkhole would swallow us up right now. It looked like we were the only big news of the day in England, certainly on social media. Our online audience was hanging on by a click, waiting patiently for any word about Molly's delivery. Brian had phoned most people after we had returned from the hospital Saturday afternoon. I could not bear to be so public about her death so soon, I was still waiting to wake up myself.

Within five minutes of meeting the hospital Chaplain, we knew it had to be one of the most powerful and positive experiences to date. Steve had a rare gift. He leaned inwards and encouraged us to all huddle together in an unbroken circle. I cradled Molly tight within my arms, all our eyes were closed. Quickly, I became aware of a bright light surrounding us, followed by a different warmth than the humid heat of August. Dominant frequency sounds were still tweaking and audible in my ears, my head perhaps being fine-tuned by a blind cranial angel. Steve hugged all three of us, as he said his prayer in whispered tones. He gave Molly her official name and his blessing. Momentarily we all cried, even me, then I composed myself back to a strong, fearless woman, deeply enraged that I had been robbed of being a mother. I was a woman who could usually withstand any amount of upset, after all, I had degrees and PhDs in failures, disappointment, and survival.

The afternoon of the 13th of August, we said farewell to Molly, until we could see her again after the post mortem when her body would be returned. This alone kept me going, as she was still somewhere in Berkshire. I asked the bereavement nurse if I could have her BA/BY grow returned unwashed, she said this would be no problem. Finding an outfit for her funeral was not easy, even though no one would ever see it. My previous career as a fashion stylist came to the fore as we headed into Reading's Oracle. Brushing past expectant mothers, new mothers test-driving eye-wateringly expensive pushchairs, new mothers with their loving older mothers who were grandmothers, (some were clearly younger than me), I stood amongst generations of triumphant mothers. I was a ghost to them all, while my wandering hands found a stunning little chiffon dress.

Normally I would have winced at the cost of something so small costing so much. But today, this was the only dress I would ever buy Molly. It had a white, embroidered daisy, scooped neckline, to hide her post mortem scars, along with a newborn cap with little silver stars to cover her slightly crushed skull. A knitted white cardigan had to go with these, with long white ankle socks, that looked like trainers. My job that day was to cover up all her defects with dignity. Meanwhile, her seven-pound body lay exposed on a mortician's stainless-steel table. I kept thinking that any moment now I would wake up, and it would still be two weeks earlier, excited that I was to have a miracle baby in a handful of days.

FOUR

Glimpses of the other side,
reflecting hopes and dreams
Deep within they now reside,
becoming masters of the scenes.

The soul is all we take with us after we die, it is our universal passport, retaining every experience about our journey in a body. We are all born, we all die, but not everyone gets to live in between. There are many times when tiny souls work through utero, wiggling their way to being newborn, determined to master toddlerhood when it has already been decided they must go back. For those left behind, there are no words, it takes extraordinary parents to endure such heartache. Harsh lessons are learnt, outdated regulations need to be reviewed, for new guidelines to be made. Inevitably, there is a closing down or an opening up of the heart, pain is experienced on all levels.

Every child lost to kin and Earth, always returns to the love of those in the Heavens. Where his/her individual mission completed. The gateway of death welcomes us all home. When a soul self-departs from warm deceased flesh, the silver cord of connection breaks above our crowns with a loud snap, freeing our spirit-stories to soar into the atmosphere. Regardless of the amount of time we spend on Earth, I believe we descend from a place where every living soul today has once existed. Yet, ironically, as a collective, no one apart from those rare gifted few, remembers a single second. No surprise that I always wondered; Who am I? Where did I come from? What was I doing here?

During my second profession as a film medic, I often found myself on the set, for when cast and crew members felt unwell, or as a precaution in case some mishap should occur. It was fascinating, watching the stories unfold in front of my ringside seat. Fantasy or reality was the open-ended question, as writers, producers, directors, cast and crew came together to bring life to the silver screen. I was always the silent observer until I realised that perhaps I was also in a film of my own making, imagining that the ancient concept writers spared no expense as they presented me with the initial script for my life story. I contemplated my invitation to return to Earthland, unfolding much like a high-end budget film production and I was ready to read my part and meet some key characters.

The Scene:

Fleeting insights recall there is no physical body in the place before Earthland; instead, love housed within a cylindrical sphere called an orb, flitted around in 'Whereverwood.' Snuggled safely within our circles of light, racing around the cosmos through an epoch of fables and parables, weaving back and forth between past and future timelines. We were not raindrops, specks of dust or the flash of the camera bouncing off a wet surface, appearing in debatable photographs, we were spirit.

Before my next life began, I would swoop under starlight, drawing into my knowledge banks all of history's greatest achievements, devastations, and untold forgotten stories. Daily, before the sun fell into its scheduled celestial spheres, I flew high up into the glittering planetary nebula, leaping through tangerine hues of stratocumulus clouds as if riding bareback upon the soft coats of Peruvian alpacas. Of course, it is impossible to explain what it is really like inside Heaven's Gates, but from all reports, it would be safe to say it is magnificent.

Around January 1966, meticulous planning and preparation of my creation began. The High Council of wise planetary Great Grand Elders summoned me in for a return to Earthland meeting. I was to research and revise my entire back catalogue within the Anamnesis consciousness memory vaults. This is where all the lives ever lived were documented in microscopic detail by our Mesopotamian secretaries. It included everything I did or did not do and the many repeated fears I overcame or continued to run from. Also, there were my personal and worldly disasters I survived, my reactions to isolated incidents that went unnoticed by the living, including all triumphs, and failures, during history's darkest times. Personality characteristics were documented, as were body images, skin tones, genders, the complex DNA mutations, all the opportunities either accepted or thoughtlessly declined. My many enemies had been logged, the debts I did not repay and, likewise, those sneaky few who still owed me were noted. Everything built up, from an idea or completed masterpieces destroyed on a reckless whim, had been recorded. File upon file of random thoughts, which could be a crushing experience to hear back millennia later.

Whoever we once were, eventually we return to Heaven's expiration centres, where a personal debrief is essential after every life has ceased. A visit to this grand palace, where the memory vaults reside in an infinite space located in the downtown districts of the Heavens, is by far a great day out for any old soul back in town. Each visit was either a complete surprise or a shock and grave disappointment, discovering all over again who you once were. Telepathy transmits hundreds of past lives in every language, even if you do not wish to hear it. This type of screening picks out previous habits, personality traits, the good, the bad, the weird and beautiful, the darn right stupid and those rare genius moments that come around once every few lifetimes. Avidly I watched frame by frame, sometimes the more successful ones were projected, lives worthy of high praise for the completion of good, honest work. Dear folk raised a tankard or two of something fermented in my honour, and kin and fellow, were genuinely saddened at my untimely departure. This kind of acclaimed death elated the big bosses in Heaven's end-of-life departments, who were very relieved to see a contract well executed.

My stories documented lifetime after lifetime, as I roamed Earthland, looking for simplified answers to complicated questions. I travelled from conception to cremation, birth to burial, tirelessly weaving through particles of time, carefully creating a bountiful tapestry of prismatic soul experiences. Some lives inspired my cobbling together of pitiful, almost lame points of view based on rhetoric or hearsay, and in others, I would proudly speak out with harsh, strong opinions based on proven truth and facts. Founded on this past life insight, my attitudes either got me killed or made me a respected leader.

Somewhere in the past, between ego and enlightenment, I tried navigating humanity's true meanings. This process resulted in different outcomes; being hurled backwards in development, becoming choked on greed, many a time drowning in self-pity, deafened by madness, almost always infuriated by politics, yet again frustrated and singled out by birth-right religions. Seconds before each physical human death, whether of natural causes, killed by accident or murdered, images of one's real purpose are projected in ones' third eye. Suddenly, there was either a smog grey mist or an aurora of colour. It was revealed that the experiences I had just lived had been in ignorant denial and darkness, as many cried with joy at each untimely passing, or there had been lifetimes where pristine progress had been achieved, where I became lighter in density.

The standard rule within every existence was to birth alongside a placenta of universal truths. For me, this usually meant a life of indoctrination into various faiths, beliefs, or staunch religions which became a shared journey for most. This experience of multi-faith options might be compared to wearing new shoes. At first many of them crippled, until they were broken in, a few seemed just about bearable, some felt regionally fashionable. In contrast, others were beneficial and even lifesaving by design. Occasionally I stumbled upon the most perfect pair of comfortable shoes, where daily life was a gentle stroll in the park. On the other foot, when tragedy struck, it was easier not to believe, running away with bare feet as fast as I could.

Once all my relevant jams and jubilance for the next life had been reviewed, it was advised I should return to Earthland during the time of the latter twentieth-century evolution. Shoehorning my cultivated spirit into a new physical design, structured for the more modern-day female body, I felt ready for the part.

The Plot:

At the time I was to be born, the world would start to move forward with incredible speed, affecting transportation, medicines, communication, artificial intelligence, and senior citizens. This world would need a new ordinance, louder female voices, especially during its dwindling stages of Piscean-led masculinity. Current Earthland behaviours would require a full and thorough review during this next scheduled generational rotation. The Great-Grand-Elders agreed I must now return as female, to be a part of a new evolution of womankind. My mission was to send subtle driblets of fresh new ideas, the examinations of all new possibilities, and positivity through the dormant veins of many redundant self-believers, through my own very detailed, yet authentic, storylines.

During this new era of evolution, the flames of women's liberation will finally be ignited. The contraceptive pill will be a new choice for women. The Second World War had indeed only just passed us by. Since the war effort, women of all ages now have a taste of working for their country and for themselves. It felt only natural that the female role I was to be born into, wanted to achieve even more during this new exciting time of equal post-war opportunities and feminine evolution, but the challenge of balancing career and family life would be tested. The new age of Aquarius and the universe itself, will urge all women to be it, then write about it, speaking it louder than ever before and take things much further than any man could ever have imagined twenty years ago, but what was, 'it?'

This was the script. I was to learn it verbatim, but allowed to ad-hoc throughout, as it would be 'my life.' I was to stand on my own two feet as a woman and go it alone for most of this next storyline. Appropriate parents had been cast on my behalf, confirmed, and approved, for their complicated ongoing shared history within a selection of previous selves. I researched day and night, by watching many seasons of us all on memory playback, analysing then noting down every moment we shared. Overwhelmed as a daunting feeling of dread dimmed my eternal inner glow, my merciless team of evolved casting and production Elders, did not believe in making room for any self-pity. They were focused on results and wanted our collective debts paid off for good, like the ruthless investors they were. My soon-to-be parents were individually unemotive and non-patrimonial. They would help me to work harder than ever on a few remaining scenes. This birth family would create a healthy, robust body for me to inhabit, yet they would try hard throughout my childhood to weaken it. Subtly, they would chip away at my strong-minded female character, paying little parental attention to my developing needs. Yikes, being the lead in my own production, was not looking glamourous.

The Department of Terms & Conditions:

The terms and duration of service for being born female, circa 1967, came via the curator of timelines and achievements. His job was to point out all the practical details for my new life ahead, my job was to listen, then in parts to tweak then agree! "My dear one, you know what's coming. I can only apologise; you have been sent the brief and thoroughly researched every detail I presume?" At least he was honest, but then again, every soul here is honest, what is the point of lying? "Yes sir, I have been made fully aware of what is to come." My next role in life was not going to be a smooth ride, but it sounded exciting in places. He continued. "This next placement has deep karmic complications, and we feel it is now time you dealt with them."

"Let me expand. Your initial key negatives have to do with abandonment, neglect, and therefore trust issues, so these parents are perfect for you. As grown-ups, they will be unreliable and erratic in their behaviours. To complicate matters, and irritate further, you will be born seeing things completely differently from them, which they will not tolerate. My dear one, you must always voice your opinions, loud and proud. This will baffle and even annoy the more recent war generations; you will pay a high price for your honesty. Please remember, this vision, this voice of yours will be a gift." All sorts of scenarios ran through my mind.

"As a child, you will be aware that you can see and feel things invisible and from other timelines. This will cause you great mental anguish as no one will believe you at first, in fact, not for a long time. However, you have a poetic soul, which means you change terrible situations into something more bearable for others in pain to understand. This will come through your abundance of creativity. You will think in shapes, formations and be truly guided by words and rhythms." This last bit made my next life sound romantically enchanting, a cross between Fanny Mendelssohn Hensel and Harper Lee. "Now then, you must be true to your ideals and visions. Your dreams will be uniquely designed visual blueprints, which we will project under déjà vu daytime visions and during your night rest, so you do not ever forget your direction."

"We aim to coordinate your birth a year from now during the year 1967, under the astrological star sign of Aquarius, as we project your moon to be 22 Piscean 43 precisely. This will reflect all unresolved past-life issues. You see, your subconscious predisposition is very much determined by the moon's location at this time of your birth, timing is the essence. The moon's position is the clearest psychic imprint of your pasts, it is, as they say in astrological circles, your emotional reservoir. We are suggesting that you return to Earthland, as it is the correct timeline to finally purge yourself from previous unresolved psychic pain and emotional refuse. This, dear child, has gone on long enough for you and your Earthland peers. Collectively you all need to start ascension into the next dimension, as we need you in other parts of the cosmos, and soon!"

I was at a loss for words. Was this a prison sentence or the golden key to finally unlocking our collective ancient jail cells? "So, my dear one, your dreams and visions must be executed in full, it is God's will and the plan of the Universe. Try to remember it this way, we are your producers, scriptwriters, editors, and directors, you are the star. Personal timing, along with a little humour will be necessary. We have deadlines! You must be born mid-February, around the 11th to the 13th in 1967, to get this last bit of karma dealt with, understood?"

"I guess so." Big blocks of dread crashed at Jenga within my mind. "From then on you will learn to be fully independent, resourceful, and resilient by the age of sixteen; we also will give you the birth number of ONE, to assist your journey of complete independence and abounding creativity, with confidence. Fear will be your biggest enemy. It is a natural human negative, so you will not be alone there. Are we clear?"

What could I say to any of this? It seemed to be written in the stars and the moon by some keen celestial screenplay writer, awaiting an Oscar nomination! "During previous incarnations, you developed strength in all matters creative, with many great disciplines. You were a fantastic timekeeper, a time-lord no less. Devoting numerous lives to many wonderful noble causes, that helped your communities and humanity, these traits are the common thread of your ongoing journey." Impressive, I almost sounded award-winning. "Let us continue." It was so much to take in. "You will have good humour during difficult periods of personal and human struggle, perfecting self-denial as an intrinsic part of attaining your more meaningful goals. These positive traits will stay with you. OK, let us move swiftly on." All I kept thinking was, who upon divinities' Earthland will I be this time around?

"At some point, you will be sharing your observations and experiences on a global level. That is, once you have overcome lifetimes of self-confidence issues due to being highly criticised by those nearest; you have always battled on. By that time, when you are in your fifth decade, the world will be in a state of chaos, having over seven and a half billion new and returning old souls inhabiting human forms. This will be a record for us, as they will all want to hear what you have to say."

"Seven billion? Gosh, that sounds like a lot of people!" I could not compute that many souls all at once, or What would I possibly be getting into? "Yes, there are so many incarnations! The processing alone will be nearly five new lives per second, a logistical nightmare for us here. Luckily that is not my department, but we have time to plan for what is coming. We always know what is coming, and the world will be in for a big shock around that time." What did that mean, a big shock? He carried on. "Expect a sudden resurgence of new technology around the time you turn twenty-nine, remember your previous Atlantean lifetimes, you will need to dig out that forgotten data, as there is already a resurgence of soul memory from that timeline. We have set up crucial situations with key people for your learning. You will be trained in type and highway codes by the age of twenty-four, but that is only if you are brave enough to go it alone in your early teens. It is all a game of dominos. You must act when we instruct you to, it will be frightening, but if you complete this module, you will meet most of your destiny targets from then on."

"It really is, as they say, in the lap of the Gods. Your

negative points, we hope, will be few this time, although dear one, you will be human, so there is no telling. We hope you will get past childhood one hundred per cent healthy and well." What? I was having momentary reservations about this next mission.

The Contract:

I had observed that every professional film has a contract, so why not mine! "Now," he said, "the legal stuff: we, the coordinators and over seers of the Destiny Planning Department, United Kingdom branch, will be offering our full assistance 24/7, so always, and I really mean this, ALWAYS call out for help. We also communicate via telepathy, automatic writing, night dreams, talking aloud, repetitive coincidences, reputable mystics and psychics, and at times Ouija, but use that only in emergencies; thus, someone will be listening every second of every Earthland day, and we will appoint your very own expert spirit guide." This all sounded fair.

"This time, we believe a female guide is more fitting, given the times upon the next horizon of equal opportunities and feminism, that began formulating during the mid-1940s. Her name is To Keep Watch, and she has over seven hundred years of personal spirit guiding experience, the best in the business. You are blessed." Her name sounded native American, perhaps she was a shaman. I assessed that this was somewhat rare, as very few people had a female spirit guide, the standard way was to have a Native American male shaman with some fancy headdress with giant colourful feathers. I found this appropriate, considering I was to be thrown into a timeline of feminine challenges, so powerful matriarchs could emerge.

"Yes, you will have a female spirit guide, she has spent time within ancient indigenous tribes, for being one of them and for observing them. She has studied vast subjects, living all over this world and within other realms, and she has shared physical lives with you during Druid, Mayan and Atlantean times. She has been predominantly female while achieving some spectacularly heroic acts, that upon Earthland went unrecognised. To Keep Watch has so much love and compassion. Her presence is strong, so you will know she is around in your earlier life, as children see everyone. As your faith dwindles, her memory will too. However, she will continue in the background to guide you to safety, especially in birth/death/re-birth situations which will be at least once every ten years or so." Now I was really questioning some of this comeback life, while he continued to talk about technicalities.

"When personal crises appear to cripple progress, these actually will be testing you for any new strengths and skills learnt to that date. These setbacks will highlight to us any ongoing weaknesses that we at the CDPD, (the Coordinators of Destiny Planning Department), will advise you to correct your direction during sleep time. If you need further guidance, especially before a situation melts your mind or depletes your body, we will be at hand. But above all, To Keep Watch will assist with your femininity issues, keeping it in check in many male-dominated situations, as indeed there will be a few. So, no more brushing inadequacies under the magic carpet, they do not exist anymore!" Human life involved so much detailing and intricate planning, we all are connected like a spider's web to so many timelines, with so many people. This was going to be a fascinating time to be born.

Cast and Crew:

"Aside from To Keep Watch, you will also have several transition guides to help from time to time. There is a strong team who all volunteered to be of assistance to you during this crazy lifetime on Earthland, 20th/21st century AD. You have done much to help and develop these grateful souls over many millenniums, so this is their final payback to you." He did not look up from his mountain of files that resembled sandcastles of liquefied light. My new name shone out backwards from each tier.

"We appoint a family liaison guide, a medical and midwife angelic team, a highly artistic creative guide, who will double up to be your angel of utter joy. Please take full advantage of this energy. We have selected a firm and solid male Gatekeeper, he will deal with many dark annoying entities, dishonest soothsayers, some sages, and general scammers that you will meet along the way. His job is to keep you safe from malevolent forces. He will be your connection to this world, and this world's connection to you." And so, with a small army of love and support ready for our next mission, I was part of a team. "Yes, OK." I understood as this was not the first mission-filled life I had lived.

"I do not wish to see you again in this office, dear child, for at least a hundred years. So, no funny business, thinking you can sneak back at any time, it is not your will to return here. So, my dear one, it is time you nailed this life. Do you wish to know your new name?" Of course, I wanted to know! "Claire, spelt with an I and an E! It means clarity and clear vision." This name rolled off his tongue and mine, the vessel of vision. A simple syllable, yet a solid, reliable name. "Now Claire, you must learn to think, feel, imagine, and create, to use that 'I' wisely, and the 'E' carefully, moving ever forward to the spheres of greater oneness, agreed?"

"Agreed!" As our chat ended, it felt like the right time to return, by the sounds of things my specific brand of consciousness was really needed. "OK then, let's make it official, please sign here and here." He stamped the papers with three blinks of muted light. My individual contract had been verified; it was now out of my hands. That meeting was recorded and filed within the Anamnesis

Vaults by a Mesopotamian secretary. The original script to my new life was complete and transferred to the relevant departments for consciousness approval, then on to the baby designing departments. The theatre was full of onlooking guides, guardian, arch, and the newly-dead training angels, all eager to earn their wings. They could see this mission clearly from high up in the Galactica, and deep down within the depths of every planetary core. The synopsis was now written in indelible ink. "Always remember, love overcomes everything. Love is love, look out for the numbers one and twenty-two, do your very best and don't ever give up."

"Finals are done, camera ready, quiet on set, roll sound and ACTION!"

FIVE

Returning from the ancient realms,
to feast on their legion of fears.

During the fifties, Rita, my mother to be, was a mere fourteen years old. She had decided to leave Austria, her motherland, the only place she ever knew, to go in search of her estranged mother Anna. Even though through no fault of her own, Grandma Anna had abandoned Rita at the age of five, she had not forgotten her, and still sent cash and parcels back home. Grandma Anna had moved to England to find cleaning work, just after the Second World War ended. She saw no future in Austria since unemployment and economic depression had crippled her country and its people. They had been devastated as a nation and morale was at its lowest. By the time Rita arrived in London, Grandma Anna had remarried a British man and had moved on. It was apparent from the start that mother and daughter did not understand, nor particularly like each other's company. Not because of their inadequate use of the English language, but because Rita simply did not know nor understand Grandma Anna, so they fought all day long in their mother tongue. On Rita's sixteenth birthday, she found a bit of independence at Peter Jones, in the shoe department on the King's Road, Chelsea. This is where she met her best friend, Brenda; they regularly went out dancing at the jazz clubs. This is also where Rita met the dashing Arthur, my dad-to-be.

In June 1965 my penniless, twenty-one-year-old Austrian, Earthland mother Rita, had just married my conservative, thirty-three-year-old British father, Arthur. This ensured her financial security for life, she never needed a paying job again, as her place, stereotypical of the time, was within the home. Her primary role from 1965 onwards was to be a stay at home wife to Arthur. Post-war personality traits were being skillfully crafted and settling nicely into the current strands of DNA. Everything was ready, for the new generation of post-post-war babies to be born during the sixties and seventies, to withstand the worst of their frustrations.

Rita's new life with her English husband meant her official status was British homemaker. She kept house while listening to awful oompah-pah, yodelling music, which reminded her of her birthplace. She cooked veal schnitzel with duchess potatoes, drank Cointreau from a sewing thimble, as she stuck millions of Green Shield Stamps into booklets, which were worth a small fortune on the open market at the time. Rita, now in her twenties, adored anything Elvis, to the point of big-crush hysteria, and had somehow become interested in the esoteric and mystical. She regularly dabbled with the Ouija board, as if it was an exclusive phone system to the heavens. She did her best at reading the tarot cards, convincing herself she was receiving messages about her future from reliable dead sources. Still, her terrible use of English gave very mixed signals on both sides of the ether, which caused hauntings and arguments along the way. Rita's fluency was in character assassination, in both Austrian and Pidgin English, so in time, she upset everyone with her condemnatory opinions.

Arthur was born in 1931, in Norwich, Norfolk not far from the seaside. He started early life as an engineer with the RAF, posted for many years in South Africa. By the time his career in the forces ended, he had married young while living abroad. All anyone knew about his first wife was that she was a lot of fun, they drank and danced all night long in the jazz clubs of cities around the world. When his contract with the forces and his marriage ended, he returned to England, depressed and desperate for a new vocation and stay-at-home wife. Arthur was known as a catch; Brenda always relayed this fact while holding a fresh cup of instant coffee with full fat, lumpy cream on top, and a starry glint in her eye. He was of a firm build, six feet tall, with dark slick hair and a noticeably thinning bald patch, right along the centre of his head.

Arthur became a company director of his father's thriving business. This chemicals company, producing car products in Wandsworth, paid him rolls of hard cash during a time before decimalisation, and valued-added tax when creative accounting was still in corporate infancy. His Indian-born accountant was just one of a couple of loyal friends he had throughout his life. Arthur then bought his first house, for five hundred pounds, in Sutton in Surrey, England. He loved to drive the newest Vauxhall. Arthur was undoubtedly a man with refined tastes. Jazz music was his world, he loved snooker, gadgets, and gardening in symmetrical, straight lines. Even though there were only three channels on British TV at the time, he bought a Beta Max video recorder and recorded his programmes while he watched them in real-time.

To secure her future, Rita knew she required some children in order to complete her new role and British status. They set up home in Gander Green Lane, but Arthur was ultra-careful in the bedroom department. After many years of practice with great beauties from all over the world, married or not, he felt confident he could control any unforeseen conception events. Rita had, for some time, been overwhelmed with suicidal thoughts because she was not getting pregnant fast enough; this no doubt was my conception team bugging her to get things moving. Fortunately, she was very cooperative as she so wished to be the mother she did not have. This is where I came in! I admit it took a while to find the right combination of family as there were also several optimistic options in more desirable warmer climates, but Rita and Arthur appeared to be the perfect pair.

It was a crisp, breezy day on Earth in February 1966, when I was called to start influencing my parent's dream state, which was part of pre-production. The urgency to get things moving was evident. I began whispering directly into Rita's ears, her future daughter's name of Claire, spelt with an I, and E. My contract stated this was important for numeric balance, humanitarian influences, and United Kingdom name spelling references. This was risky since Rita was not good at spelling in English. Time was tight as I waited on standby, observing that all aspects and factors were now in near-perfect alignment for my conception. Rita became even more savaged by maternal hormonal desire; her body was in baby-making meltdown. To Keep Watch gestured I back off a bit, or it could all go wrong. It was apparent, my mother-to-be was at her most sensitive and vulnerable, but she had a plan.

Once Arthur had gone to his office for the day, Rita felt alone, not really knowing anyone nearby. All-day she listened to the radio, so she could learn more English, as she went about sabotaging all manner of contraception. The newly invented contraceptive pill was secretly popped straight down the loo. Condoms were punctured with a fine sewing needle, usually kept for special synthetics and delicate chiffon blouses. Lies were told about where in her cycle she was. This time Rita listened to me from the Heavens, as I spoke to her in mother tongue, because she still dreamt in Austrian, (spirit speaks every language).

February, then March 1966 passed us all by. To Keep Watch, and my new team frantically twiddled ethereal fingers, trying to conjure up any kind of miracle. Austria had just won the Eurovision song contest with '*Merci, Chérie*' (Thank you, darling!) Rita was beside herself with joy as she watched their brand-new colour television, half purchased with a ton of her Green Shield Stamp booklets. This invention brought out the colours of the costumes, and this gave Rita a great idea.

April 1966 became the final deadline for a British conception and my new journey. Saturn, the planet of change, and Neptune, the planet of ideas and visions, were in resourceful flow, and of great value to Rita's impossible mood swings. Arthur had no clue that such a detailed plan, for him to become a dad, was even in motion. The first week in May was pushing it, but it happened, conception by articulate maternal deception. Arthur was fast approaching forty and still very set in his bachelor ways. The announcement of my arrival needed to be linked with another momentous, happy Earthland event so that he would not do something drastic, like have me aborted in a moment of paternal despair. The 1966 FIFA world cup seemed like the right time for Rita to break the news to my dad.

Reaching nine weeks gestation, my heart had been beating for twenty-one days. Rita said nothing to anyone, being pregnant suited her normal erratic mood swings, so no one suspected a thing. The World Cup football hysteria was making grown men emotional wrecks during office hours, including my normally very composed dad-to-be. I had done my homework, England was heading for a historic win at Wembley, Middlesex London, and I would then be pre-term and twelve weeks old. It seemed everyone's life plans, including my new parents, the players, the opposition West Germans, fans from both sides, bookmakers, the legendary commentators, all crossed paths at that exact moment. What a perfect time for my mother to finally break the news of my arrival when the World Cup was at fever pitch across the United Kingdom. She hoped Arthur would be too distracted to notice. England was coming home, and so was I. If my dad had thought his freedom was over before, by being married to my safe, stay-at-home mother to be, it was now!

Surprisingly, Arthur was thrilled with the happy news. I had grown into the safe second trimester, during the second week in August 1966, at thirteen weeks plus five days. Snugly, basking in my mother's amniotic-filled uterus, both parents broke the news to our extended British branch of the family, just after England had won the World Cup. The Austrian side of the family were equally thrilled too. The whole country was hysterical with positivity for weeks, if not decades after, for in that same year England also won the Eurovision song contest, with Sandie Shaw's '*Puppet on a String*.'

At forty-one weeks and one-day gestation, I could not hold back any longer. It was showtime, the very moment I had been anticipating. After thirty-six hours of exhausting wriggling and pushing on my part, Rita screamed out that she could not go on, it was all too much for her. Suddenly I felt forced into a more favourable position by To Keep Watch, and headed down the centre of the birthing canal. Open sesame, the doorway to this new life was stretched to ten centimetres by two lovely birthing cherubs. Having been assigned a superhero female spirit guide was exciting, her sole job was To Keep Watch. She squatted beside me, giving the nod if something was right or if it was wrong, which I felt within my evolving gut of instinct. Her job was to step in if I was in life-threatening danger. To be honest, this life business was a bit much already, and I had not even drawn my first breath yet. She would wag her finger and shake her head, implying for me not to give up. Suddenly, on the other side of the tunnel, cold metal branches waited to encase my head, making me queasy. With a final yank of metal forcing me into this world, two days before Valentine's Day I finally arrived. It was the 12th of February, 1967 at 03.35 a.m.

Notes were immediately written upon flip charts that I was female. The midwife wrapped me up within a crocheted blue blanket. My mother insisted I be named Claire, spelt with an I and an E, a name that meant clear vision and clarity. My name, ironically, would bring about a very ambiguous future. Weighing in at a hefty 9 lbs and 4 oz, I suddenly felt the heavy weight of physical density. Instantly all memory of the heavens faded. I had no recollections of who I had been, arriving here, unsure of who I was to become.

Dad stayed up all night so he could be present at my Sunday dawn birth. He held his firstborn child in his tailored suited arms, surprisingly overwhelmed, as fatherly love radiated from his heartline down into his long fingers, as he carefully counted mine. In those days, this was the nearest thing to skin-to-skin contact. After a little while, he handed me back to the midwife, who immediately placed me in a plastic nursing cot. A name tag had been attached to my wrist; this was evidence I had landed on this planet. Half-starved, they failed to connect me to my mother's bosom, as they wheeled me into another room, next to a radiator, as February snow was predicted. I felt miles away from the only heartbeat I knew well, banished from the placenta I once snuggled, far from the womb where I had happily resided. For the first few hours of my existence, they left me alone in that sterile plastic box, while they attended to my exhausted mother. I had to accept that the respected Great Grand Elders had handpicked this mother for me. Her role was to birth me, the nurturing, guiding, protection and unconditional love parts were missing from day one, as she did exactly what her life contract told her to do.

Later that same day of my birth, *'I'm a Believer'* by The Monkees reached number one in the UK hit parade, setting the stage to be the soundtrack to my new life. If I had just waited three weeks, my soundtrack could have been *'Please Release Me, Let Me Go,'* by Engelbert Humperdinck.

Unfortunately, just after my second birthday, my parents had also made twin sisters. Identical, screaming demons had invaded my world of exclusive parental domination. I was just beginning to master the art of toddlerism. I wondered when Rita and Arthur ever had the energy to make more babies? I felt sure I had been utterly exhausting for them both. This was the moment when I had to learn to stop needing. From the age of seventeen months, I was already on my way to wearing big girl's pants, which would have helped Rita out a lot once the twins were born. Now, between double nappy changes and potty training, my world was not the only one that had been turned upside down.

Amid the tumult of motherhood, Rita found herself a new hobby in haberdashery and dressmaking. Inspired directly from Peter Jones dress patterns, she recreated not one, but three of everything. She did not understand that I was born to appreciate style, on top of this wardrobe humiliation, we also all wore the same sensible, matching wide-fitting Clarke's shoes. This continued until I reached the age of fifteen, and resulted in many socially awkward situations. Although Arthur was usually original when it came to buying for himself; annually, he likewise purchased three of the same Christmas gifts for his girls. We were treated the same, no favouritism or acknowledgement of individualism. That was fine for twins, but I longed to fulfil my separate birth path. I knew instinctively that I had a different mission than my sisters, but this first bit of the journey was going to have to be the same as theirs.

Alongside many throat, tonsil, and pharynx flare-ups, I had mumps three times. All these upper body viral and bacterial mutations had, no doubt, developed from never being able to voice anything. It was an unspoken rule that I did not speak until spoken to, and I should have zero expectations that anyone would listen to me. My mother successfully silenced any unnecessary infant chattering or crying for whole days at a time, by force-feeding bottles of infant liquid Paracetamol, making me constantly drowsy and slightly drooly, and in time, addicted to sugar. During one lethargic afternoon, Brenda felt it only right to call an ambulance. Rita pleaded for her not to call 999, in case the authorities threw me into Barnardo's home for orphans, but her real fear was that Arthur would stop her housekeeping money and quickly move on to wife number three. Brenda reluctantly agreed with her, and to her final days regretted her decision. She always finished telling me this story with, "Claire, lord forbid when I think back, you could have died, but thank God you didn't!"

I had consistently been sent home from school with every kind of throat complaint. Whatever the illness, Rita met me wearing her neutral, non-maternal expression. As soon as our backs were turned from concerned teachers, with clenched teeth and a forceful hand resting on the back of my head, she marched me back to the house. Once home, my feverish self was banished to my bland single bedroom. The real problem was, whenever I became sick, it was a further inconvenience for my mother. My unexpected presence disrupted her valuable childfree time, where she was busy homemaking, while sneakily smoking packets of cheap supermarket fags. The only clear windows she had during her housewife's week, were the new modern aluminium double-glazed ones, which Dad had installed, due to the extended fuel crisis of 1973.

SIX

Welcome to the witching hour
Where the hands of age run slow.

Arthur was fast becoming dumbed down by family life in general, especially with three daughters and his second wife, who notably displayed ad hominem tendencies within every argument. His inner bachelor was progressively dying a slow and painful demise into inevitable domesticity. He had enough of London's city life, so he decided to move us all and his thriving chemicals business to Grantham, Lincolnshire. This was rumoured to be the next up-and-coming postcode to live north of London. He bought a detached four-bedroom house, with front and back gardens, where he planted evergreens within symmetrically square, bricked boxes. His lawn was cut to perfection, with neat lines like Court One at Wimbledon.

For me, this tricky move north with no familiar friends or family nearby, plus starting a new school at the age of five, was a big wrench thrown into my life's script. Thanks to my awful haircut which my mother styled into the shape of an Arcopal lotus bowl, which was a popular tableware choice of its time; I became a target to my peers. My unfortunate lankiness made me tower over the tallest boys in my class, which certainly compounded my problems. I hated school life already, and there were eleven more gruelling years left to go.

Brenda always described Arthur as 'rather handsome.' A successful company director with three full-time employees, some cracks were already showing, as the overwhelming stress of being a full-time husband and father was diminishing him by the second. He decided to stop smoking forty Rothmans a day, while every morning at dawn, he put himself through a yoga routine, blaming it on a middle-age crisis. Behind closed doors, he sipped on hot water and lemon which aided digestion, and practised sun salutations upon a foam mat, placed respectfully upon the new beige shag pile carpet. If we ever disturbed his core bodi-balance, he shouted through the closed door to "leave him the hell alone," thereby confirming his more complicated 'dusk' personality was still dominating his emerging 'spiritual dawn' persona.

Arthur was always a keen jazz musician; he had played at many music venues during the last couple of decades. Just after we sat down together to eat our family evening meal, we usually endured 'dad rants' that none of us understood. He would then swiftly excuse himself, disappear into his self-built music room to practice his saxophone or clarinet. The room looked more like a Chinese takeaway; thanks to the cheap teak-looking panelling he had installed himself almost everywhere. Here he proudly housed his vast collection of vinyl records, each disc loved, cherished, and cared for better than we were. Every slice of sound lovingly snuggled within protective plastic sleeves, filed in alphabetical order, just in case one of his babies got lost. His evening tipple would be a large Teacher's scotch and water, sometimes with two clanking rocks of ice in the summertime, as he reclined back into a cream coloured, retro, egg swivel chair, listening to the likes of Duke Ellington and Benny Goodman. Heavy vinyl played on the best music centre, with real diamond stylus. He taught little Claire the importance of balancing sound by standing the speakers high up from the floor, each one spaced equally apart, for the perfect auditory experience.

One Saturday afternoon, Dad had bought a new album from a music shop in Nottingham, and as he put it on, I curled myself up next to his slippered feet under the swivel egg chair. When hearing the sounds, a sudden jolt of pure emotion surged from within my belly, which made me sob. Acker Bilk's *Aria* still triggers emotional outbursts to this day. With a sense of urgency and devotion to music, he encouraged me to play any musical instruments at all. Trying the clarinet first, because he had one, we attempted to duet together while he played sax. This somewhat worked, but it was apparent that I could not read a note of music. At that moment, Arthur realised that I had a musical ear. Despite owning all this natural musical talent, little Claire just wanted to paint and draw while listening to any kind of music. This obstinate pre-teen defiance of his wishes upset him greatly. He had grand musical fantasies, in which I would play alongside him at Ronnie Scott's in Soho London, or tour the world with the London Symphony Orchestra, as he was a huge Star Wars fan.

"Claire, why don't you want to play music like me, you are such a natural?" Arthur pleaded. "Because, I want to draw. Can I not do both?" I felt rather adult in my response. "That is not what I meant. I can hear how talented you are at music; you do not even need to read a note, that is a gift. Trust me, you will not make a bean from drawing pretty pictures. Where is there any money in drawing? Drawing is a hobby like my music is a hobby, no one draws who doesn't have a proper job on the side to pay their bills." My part-time jazz dad sounded like he knew what he was talking about, as he had never made any money playing jazz music, not since I was born. I imagined, deep down, that this was the one big regret of his, as he was never happy in his day time job.

"Claire, you need to touch base in this world. You constantly live in a fantasy reality, there are no decent jobs in drawing. I am trying to teach you something here, but as always, you know best." I was eight years old. I did not need a job, my world was drawing, painting, and cutting up the hideous clothes my mother continued to make, fashioning them to look more like my own. This usually evaporated Rita into one of her red mists. I understood Arthur's 'real world' all right; it was boring, controlling, and lonely. Everything felt very adult miserable. I vowed never to get a proper job, get married, or have any damn kids if this is how miserable it was going to be.

Within a handful of years living in this new town, I could sense strain at home. We saw our Grandparents and Brenda maybe twice a year, but my parents did not seem to have many new friends, no one came to the house. Every weekday, Arthur returned from the office precisely at five thirty-two, pouring himself a very large scotch. With high drama, he picked apart everything that had upset him that day, from some story on the news to rants about people from other countries in general. This seemed a bit unusual, as he had lived in South Africa for many years and married a white South African lady in the fifties. His trusted accountant and lifetime friend was Indian, he loved to eat curries at the curry house, and Chinese food in the marketplace. His current wife was Austrian, and his three daughters were now half European. His life was extremely multicultural for the times, including his love for music, which was undoubtedly borderless. Maybe there was nothing much to complain about during this time.

Being the most argumentative of everyone, I always found myself being the hot topic for his anxieties, as my Aquarian make-up continuously defended the underdog, without understanding a thing about what an underdog was in the first place. Dinner time was not the best family time together. I learnt how to eat as fast as I could, leaving enough time between every mouthful to share my interesting opinions and maybe slip in some genius ideas across to the entire family, none of them motivated in the slightest, about my points of view. My unengaged audience was simply not absorbed in anything to do with being alive. I tried in vain to explain, in the best pre-pubescent way I could, of how this world worked. After being told I knew nothing at my age, I was promptly sent up to my bedroom for the night with no television. My room became my creative hideout, so that suited me just fine.

Every Thursday evening, all through the British summer months, I was unwillingly dragged to the Spiritualist Church in town by my supernatural-curious mother. The congregation of 'the nearly dead,' welcomed me to the group. A very old couple instructed me to sit down in the middle of their coven of faith healing pensioners. Seated upon a tall wooden stool, my socked feet were firmly anchored on top of the itchy tiled carpet, that cut through socks to bare feet. My eyes stayed half-closed, linking both thumbs together on my lap, I knew the unspoken rule of spiritual healing was no touching. Still, I could feel strong heat-like energy, that of many people, touching me at once all over my body. Squinting one eye, I saw the outline of two people snapping their arthritic fingers in the air over my head like flamenco dancers, wiping things away that were not there in the first place. They swayed and hummed, claiming to heal my inner badness in return for a weekly donation from Rita's housekeeping money.

On one occasion, I thought rude words like bloody and bugger, mimicking my parents who said this a lot to each other, even though it was directed at us when we were driving them nuts. I thought swearing would test if these perceived lunatics could read minds. It seemed they really could. In unison, they abruptly took their hands away from my possessed auric field, gasping for breath, my badness was sucking the oxygen from their failing lungs. Standing back, they claimed that nothing more could be done for me. This was not the response my frustrated mother was after. Ashamed that I had shown her up; she grabbed my upper arm and dragged me back to the brand-new blue Cavalier.

The only games I played with Rita were telepathic mind games, we never once talked to each other like a mother and daughter should. We did the Ouija board, where there were no dice, no cards or prizes, no winners, and no losers. She insisted I had a different 'special gift' from the musical gift my dad thought I possessed. I became very good at answering her questions to the spirit worlds. At first, this infuriated Rita, and she claimed that I was an obstinate know-it-all, this was the one big word she had learnt while playing Scrabble with my dad. She believed I had been earwigging while she chatted on the cream GPO 746 rotary kitchen wall phone, but then she heard me say things aloud that no one knew but her. The plastic disc slid all over the board, spelling out her answers in both languages, which I understood. I thought Rita was pushing the disc, she thought I was pushing it. I wondered if she had been playing some sort of amusing spelling game for my benefit until, on second thought, I questioned if she was smart enough to think of such a thing. I did not win at this Ouija game; my spirit felt vanquished by using all these unique gifts in that negative way, which gave me terrible nightmares. Our house became haunted, our family dynamics felt cursed from that time on. I consciously shut down any hoodoo or musicality fortes I may, or may not have possessed.

SEVEN

My souls been burnt, singed on bitter truths.

After the lockdown of all my talents, which seemed necessary to stop my parents from arguing, things soon got nasty. Rita raged in her native parlance, but no one ever understood a word of what she said when she was in those moods. She became unreadable in any language, as she sought advice from new friends from beyond the grave through visiting mystics, who foretold in the cards that I was leaving home very soon. Rita demonstrated her daily frustrations through the art of mime, by pouring Arthur's bottles of whiskey down the kitchen sink, including his secret stash generally hidden in the coal shed. Rita's eyebrows were at their highest peak cresting above her ice-blue eyes, her misunderstood tongue poking into her right cheek, she finished off with a 'humph' and a firm nod. In retaliation, Arthur hummed his annoyance aloud, and crushed all her cheap supermarket cigarettes down the same plughole; our plumbing must have been shot to pieces. Arthur literally hid away in his music room night after night, and all day on weekends. The worst part was hearing him turning the key in the lock, so I could not listen to his music with him anymore. We lost him during this time, as he spent long hours at the office, except for Monday evenings, which he spent in the snooker halls. Suddenly, this was not about me anymore.

This was also a very challenging time of radical sexual equality protests and Women's Rights rallies in the world. In 1975, the United Nations had declared an International Women's Year by organising the first World Conference for Women, held in Mexico City. In the United Kingdom, the Sex Discrimination Act 1975 was brought in as law. Women everywhere wanted more rights, more opportunities to finally voice their opinions, in the hope of, one day, being accepted as equal to men.

During 1976 my parents split up. It was Rita that moved out, not me. In a way, I was relieved as, at the age of nine, I had no job or life skills to support myself. This proved those annoying card readers were all a bunch of witchy-woo liars. She rented a room on the other side of town. Our separated mother's board and lodgings had no place for us to sleep; even if there had been, it would have cost more money to rent extra rooms. We stayed at home with Dad, who had already torn out what was left of his thinning hair. After a few days of maternal abandonment, it became evident that Arthur did not have a clue how to be a house husband, but neither did he wish to admit how much his stay-at-home wife really did in the home.

Our eating patterns changed dramatically. Firstly, there were no arguments over the dinner table, since my dad did not know how to cook a sausage sober, and we dared not complain, for fear there would be no dinner at all, so we rarely ate at home. Every Tuesday after school, we drove into town and had Wimpy burgers. Fish and chips were staples at the famous Windsor Fish Bar every Saturday lunch, or every other evening after school when nothing else was open. Sunday was a Chinese banquet at the Hop Sing in Westgate, where we ate Asian noodles and chicken balls with chopsticks, that were spun around on a lazy Susan; this cuisine is still my favourite. Occasionally, Arthur made us eat vindaloo curry, which is a Portuguese dish in origin, made normally from pork, marinated in wine-vinegar and garlic, with mustard seeds, a ton of fire chillies, ginger, cumin, and tamarind. What was he thinking? I was nine, it gave my entire mouth third-degree burns that felt numb for days after. After the second hurried mouthful, I should have known better, but I had gotten into the habit of eating too fast in case of any eruptions, but there were no more arguments. I had to eat the lot. There were no extra drinks to fan the flames, we were only allowed one miserly glass of Coke, in case the sugar from the Coke would give us cavities. The rest of the time, we ate whatever was in the deep freezer, which was generally well-stocked because an older woman came around twice a week to refill it.

This emotional separation dragged on for weeks. Every lunchtime, Rita met the three of us at school. She would inspect every inch of me. Leaning forward, she spat at my dirty uniform, aiming right at the encrusted food dried in from three days before, picking it all off with her bendy calcium-deficient nails, until it looked passable. Her interrogations would start by subtly asking what Arthur had been up to? "Nothing." I replied, which was not the whole truth. "Nossing, your dad has been up to NOSSING?" she continued. "We play Atari-pong on the telly, watch TV all day long at weekends, he plays his music loud so we can hear it in the garden, where I help him weed the flower beds, that's it, so nothing."

What does a nine-year-old do, when repeatedly accused of lying? Dad went out a lot in the evenings, leaving us with the housekeeper, so I had no clue what he was up to outside those four walls. Rita looked almost disappointed that he had acted the brilliant father. Dad bought a special Barbie doll for me, from the family-run toy shop in the market square. I did not want to hurt his feelings by saying that I was getting far too old for dolls, and I wondered if it was a reward for my silence. He even went as far as to allow us to dress differently. I suspected this was probably due to the mounting laundry crisis, but I was grateful. Every day at school lunchtime, in that little meeting room with Rita, it was always the same. "What's your dad up to? The truth now, Claire?" Not, give us a hug I have missed you, how are you? What have you been up to? "Nothing!" I knew he was up to all sorts, I was told never to lie, but this was tricky as it was one parent against the other. Who do I side with? This stress went on for weeks, possibly months.

Running out of the school gates, expecting my regular long walk to meet Dad at the chip shop, it was a shock to see both parents sitting together in Arthur's brand-new Vauxhall Cavalier, anxiously waiting for us. They had gotten back together, explaining that the reunion was for our sakes. Thank the divorce Gods, as I could not stand to eat another cod and chips, however famous they were. I missed Rita's cooking, but I instantly knew I would miss being able to dress however I wanted, even more. Once Rita had caught up with the mountain of laundry, it was back to three of everything worn on the same days. I am sure she had obsessive-compulsive disorder. I understood that the split was, in part, because Rita wanted a job; thanks to the new and fashionable women's liberation front, however, Rita stood somewhere at the back of this movement. I believed she let herself down by not getting a job somewhere during her time away, by not standing up for her convictions when she moved out. Getting a job would have given more credence to her point of view, but what did I know about anything?

Arthur had initially not wanted her to work at all. His ancient mindset and generational programming meant that he was to pay all the household bills, as he was the provider for the family. My mother's job was to look after all of us, and he thought she could not do both. Rita left us, all to prove her point that looking after us was a thankless, unpaid job, and housekeeping was not enough compensation. Eventually, they compromised, for Arthur upped her housekeeping money, and let her work for him as his secretary, typing his invoices. His night-time music room had become Rita's daytime office, now equipped with a brand-new electric typewriter, a comfortable adjustable chair, and a red leather-bound Roberts radio, blasting hit parade songs of the seventies.

A couple of years later, any dreams of going to the local all-girls school went out the window before the second question on my eleven plus exam paper. I had fog brain, thanks to the worst cold imaginable, with a full-on snotty runny nose. As I wiped away the dribble and phlegm with one allocated single-layered tissue, just in case we had scribbled answers on it, I knew I had failed. The only option now was the comprehensive school, right on my doorstep. The downside to being eleven in 1978, was that we were forty-three girls all sheepishly entering The Central School for Boys for the first time. There was not one mature female role model to look up to in the upper years, no one to obtain vital girlie tips from, because there was only a sea of teenage boys, over three hundred of them. Not one of us in that first year had a clue how to behave as girls, let alone as young women. Our headteacher was Mrs Belvoir, a more severe Margaret Thatcher, who was also born and bred in Grantham. We were terrified of her.

I did, in fact, acquire the most wonderful form and art teacher, Mr Hull. He was to be my day time guardian. My leanings toward the more masculine traits, during this challenging adolescent time, was not due to unfortunate hairstyles, towering height, imbalances of X and Y-chromosomes, or my endocrine system in meltdown. It was due to my unfair placements within this previously all-boys school. Mrs Belvoir tried her best to teach us that normal girls do not behave in this or that way, as I continued to question how any of this was normal? I barely passed the exams by the skin of my cavity-free teeth. Daily I dealt with agonising growth surges and regular brain malfunctions, through gradual stages of adolescent stress. I struggled with compulsory bra wearing, commanding hormone spurts and too many feminine hygiene issues to keep up with. It was complicated, being a female teenager in seventies male-dominated Tory Grantham.

During this fragile time of adolescence, I was hanging on for dear life to my flagging self-esteem, everyday beating myself up by looking at my image in the mirror. Both parents pretended to get on with each other, while at the same time screaming blue murder at me, which was, in fact, directed back at each other. If only my blood tribe could speak the same language. I was regularly banished to my bedroom, where I happily drew many pictures and dreamt of living the life of an artist.

One miserable Thursday evening, I was sitting beneath the creaking staircase at the Spiritualist Church waiting for Rita. Missing *Top of the Pops*, which was the only decent programme I liked on television at the time. Dad refused to record any of it on his precious Betamax, saying it was my kind of nonsense programmes and videotapes cost a fortune. I patiently waited for my mother, as she balanced upon the wooden stool in the sky-blue healing room next door. My secret hope was that the creepy nearly dead were using their magic fire fingers to thaw out Rita's inner icebergs. Staring right at me was a copy of *Nursery World 1977*. Flicking through the crumpled pages, I saw there were adverts in the back from parents who needed to foster out their own children. Intrigued, I sat and studied the ads and wondered why a parent would want to give their progeny away? Sensing Rita's aphotic auric field coming to find me, I stuffed the magazine under my brown school anorak, which she still made me wear after school.

The protests and punishments were in full flow, as I stood alone, a hormonal teenage suffragette, a pubescent abolitionist. I was pro-healthy discussions, but also pro-peace, pro-people. I became a Monday-to-Friday demonstrator fighting to bring down our family wall of restrictions, hypocrisy and lies. My only issue was, no one understood nor listened to me. I was a seven-day prisoner held captive in my bedroom. Summoning in the spirit of Houdini himself, I asked if he could help to identify all hidden escape opportunities that my parents had not thought through. Once free, I ran towards the town centre where my friends from school used to hang out. Some petty shoplifting and general thieving became a bit of a fugitive pastime, with a lot of lying once hunted then captured. This was blatant attention-seeking behaviour, due to low self-esteem from a lifetime of constant criticism, especially during this time of bleak parental chaos.

My eye caught sight of a black and white geometric t-shirt in a shop window in town. Without thinking, I went in to claim it. I entered the single cubicle to try it on, with no intention of paying for it. My heart was pounding from my chest as I threw it on under my fur rimmed parker coat, then ran out of the shop. The desperation to wear retail had reached critical. I had no pound notes to pay for this strand of rebellion; but, by this point, I did not care about the consequences. A prison cell sounded more appealing than my bedroom.

Sneakily I entered by the back door, hurrying past both parents as they sat at the kitchen table, competitively playing the British version of Scrabble. Nothing got past my eagle-eyed mother and her single woman detective agency. Her heightened sense of smell set off alarm bells as she caught a whiff of brand-new retail fabric. Charging up the floral wallpapered staircase in hot pursuit, she burst into my room through the door, which comically bounced back off the wall, into her face. After hours of interrogation, of torturous screeching and beatings, she backed me into the far corner of the room, her tones drilling holes into my head. I was near breaking point. In front of my accused self was my guardian angel defence team, all shaking their heads in dismay as I prayed to come up with viable excuses, while the storm continued to rage inside this delicate little teacup. Rita shouted accusations like the lead prosecution barrister at the International Court of Justice in the Hague, she summed up every individual crime committed in my short life thus far. I had, without a doubt, blatantly stolen it from somewhere, this was a crime! It was indeed a crime, but it was a cry for help even more, but my cries fell on deaf ears, instead I was punished severely.

Adolescence under my parents' ruling, became Guantanamo. My heart started to connect with the fascinating rhythms of other tribes. Each year, as I grew up, music was becoming more arresting and fashions more exciting; men looked like girls, girls looked like boys, and whoever created these looks were geniuses. Unfortunately, not one boy at our school looked remotely like a girl, although a lot of girls started to look more like boys. Sadly, for me, Grantham lagged behind London trends. I was born a Londoner, a budding trendsetter if I was only given a chance. My family had its own tribal issues, Homo-neanderthalensis had evolved faster than our current family dynamic during this time of juvenile and Universal change.

My safe, unadventurous mother still insisted on dressing all three of us the same, including the indestructible, wide-fitting Clarkes shoes, so as not to cripple our growing feet. My body shape changed by the second, parts of me grew outwards, upwards, and around, and I was enduring mental breakdowns alongside painful menstrual periods. Why did girls bleed in the first place?

I devoured the Encyclopaedia of the Human Body 1972 issue, (The Teenage Years), I decided there and then that I was never going to have babies if it meant going through all this every month of my life. I knew the adult Claire would be far too busy chasing big dreams, thinking up grand designs, travelling the world, making lots of money by drawing pictures, so I would have no spare time to raise a family of my own.

Towering over both twins, reaching the dizzy heights of Rita's permanently waved hair, fast catching up with Arthur's forest of dad eyebrows, I endured complicated dealings with training bras, hated deodorant and missed slinging on a white vest beneath those ghastly home-made nylon blouses. My old, familiar, comforting white vest, which also graciously stopped static dancing with my flyaway hair, was no longer in my wardrobe. I did not have a clue what my body was doing, why it behaved the way it did, or why I was behaving the way I was. Simply put, it was not clear to me who I was anymore, or who these people were who created me.

EIGHT

Built on loss, built on sorrow
We had today, but no tomorrow.

How did I ever end up with these parents in monotonous up-and-coming Grantham? I wished, somehow, I had been adopted, and they had not quite got around to telling me the truth. This thought gave me hope that my real birth parents might have settled down by now and would want me back. My impressionable spongy mind turned into a female Alan Turing, just so I could code crack their adult double meanings, which continually left me losing this war. All I wanted was to follow my order and design; little did I know at the time that this 'was' my order and design. My parents made it very clear on many occasions that neither of them understood children, nor particularly liked my developing progressive personality, which they referred to daily, as my inflated ego. I was two-thirds them, carrying all our ancestral stories through my weakening veins, the good and the bad. Perhaps their disdain was a thing of their time, and my time had not blended well with theirs quite yet.

During the early eighties, an adult could buy five hundred Paracetamols in a single, giant flip-top tub, which had been left on a white plastic bedside table for teenage kids to experiment with. Sitting cross-legged upon the lamb's skin rug by my mother's side of the marital bed,

I opened the tub of painkillers. Shaking the final twenty-three tablets in the container onto the palm of my left hand, I raised them to my mouth, munching hard on the dry, chalky pills, assisting them down with water from the bathroom tap, collected in a tie-dye plastic cup. At that moment, I could not see a future Claire as dying was the only obvious solution. After all, my mother had tried her best over the years to kill me with liquid Paracetamol, but I survived.

Alone in my bedroom, I pondered deeply about what was to come. I went through stages of anger, then surrender, then back to anger. By the time To Keep Watch got through to my flagging over-thinking consciousness, by making my nose itch with her skilful revival techniques, my internal organs were debating how long they could keep functioning without medical intervention. Then my personal medical team of angelic crusaders flew in, slapping my face to snap me out of this mental prison I had created. My breathing became rapid, light-headedness danced with dizziness through the veins of all ten fingers and toes, this was good news of sorts, as I was feeling something. Dragging every one of my drama bones down the staircase, my vision blurred through tears, left shoulder continuously rubbing against the worn-out, orange, floral wallpaper (that added to the ongoing hallucinations), which projected my imminent demise up into the planets. Politely I knocked on the oak-effect kitchen door, waiting to be asked in. Arthur and Rita chose to ignore my pleas of imminent death as they continued to calculate their next scrabble word. Their only response was telling me to "stop being so bloody dramatic and get back to your room," before one of them gave me a hiding.

Genuinely in fear of organ failure, I forced myself back up the grand staircase, rubbing the right shoulder along the same worn out stretch of seventies wallpaper. What do I do now?

I wrote my final farewell note, abandoning it on the single bed.

"To Mum, Dad, and Twins, I am done, Claire." Before long, I could feel heavy pins and needles as my breathing sped up, the painkillers took control of every extremity. Each finger felt like a sausage roll, I could not move them at all

A tapping noise came from the upstairs box-sized toilet window. One of the home-crafted crochet potpourri bags Rita had won in a raffle at a spiritualist coffee morning, blew gently in the cross breeze. Was it the spirit of Houdini assisting my escape yet again? A plan came to mind. I pushed one foot out of the cat-flap-sized window, swinging both long thin legs around, wriggling my back and bottom until both feet felt a flat surface below. From there, with the grace of Dame Margot Fonteyn, by leaping down onto the garage roof, then skydiving eight-feet to the tarmac below, I found freedom. Luckily, I had taken a heap of the painkillers, and could not feel a thing as I dragged myself up the steep driveway. Limping to the corner shop near my school, I fell to the floor. Fortunately, a girlfriend was at the shop and called an ambulance from the phone box. Fear shivered tiny sweat beads from my damp cold skin of youth, as sirens faded out into the background.

A large plastic tube plunged its way down my throat; the purpose of this was to make me wretch up the pain relief, which ironically, had been swallowed to take my pain away. I woke up fast as my throat is ultra-sensitive to everything foreign. Rita stood by the cubical screen; I guess my friend phoned her too. She said nothing. My stomach was pumped free of drugs, and breakfast cereal from that morning. I looked flushed and bloated. Once discharged, Rita dragged my hair into the car first. The night shift nurses said nothing to anyone official, as in those days, it was not their place to do so. Letters of referral were written to Mrs Belvoir at the school, and a child psychologist was appointed by the family GP but was never executed. My parents, under any form of interrogation, blatantly denied we had problems, as they fought anyone from the outside world for interfering, they were utterly convincing to outsiders. Nothing happened even though social services had been informed; no follow-ups were carried out; I was no nearer to being adopted.

Rita was getting harder to gauge. Motherhood did not suit her at all, but she wasn't a working person either. So, who was she? What was her purpose? Rita's housecoat had been made of Teflon, her non-stick persona had avoided any maternal bonding, by concealing her warmth behind a toughened shield of hidden pain. I have no memory of her holding me in any capacity of loving-kindness, my recollections are of irritation, anger, and frustration. We found no middle ground, as she never understood a single joke; not those from inside a Christmas cracker, to knock-knocks, to Ronnie Corbett's story jokes on a Saturday night. This was unnatural, as eight million other people in Great Britain alone understood the Corbett jokes. I often wondered if this was due to the language barrier, even though her accent was becoming more Lincolnshire in parts. She told me that she recently started to dream in English, which I naively thought was ridiculous. As far as I understood, everyone dreamt in English.

Dad became verbally abusive, with cutting remarks and persistent humiliations. Their previous separation had changed nothing. As I grew older, bigger, and stronger, he became more childish, belittling, and weak. His plaint was that I back chatted too much, because I did not understand things. His retaliation was to aggressively hurl insults my way, instead of explaining to a curious and inquisitive child why things were the way they were, or finding some form of common ground which was educational and fun. His inability to control himself was far more potent than any desire to raise balanced children. Was he right because he was the adult, and I was the child?

It was the early eighties and the kind of open-minded, positive free-thinking parenting that I needed, had not yet been discovered, nor discussed, nor understood by my post-war parents who bore modern-day children. Self-help books were rare to find, and when found were for mumbo jumbo sissys, and the internet was still at least two decades away for the masses. I often wondered where the softy dad went; the one who did downward dog in the early mornings, the man I cried with while listening to music, the man who dried my hair after a Sunday evening bath and made me medal-winning arts and craft pieces for school. At five foot ten, weighing eight stone (112 lbs), I now stood eye to eye with this man who created me. I had developed a protective resistance of my own, responding to his constant insults by back chatting more, with an ultra-witty retort, like a heckled comedian live on stage. It was my only coping mechanism, which sometimes broke the ice and made him laugh. This meant there was hope that he could still understand humour. Most of the time, he just became angrier. I laughed louder at every strike of his hand, which was not funny at all. At fifteen years of age, I needed less conflict, and a little more understanding and independence, but this was never going to happen.

One cold March evening, as it was beginning to get lighter after school, I took my chances, sneaking out the kitchen door, running along the main road, past the hospital, through the centre of town. My destination was my friend Sarah's house, as I knew her father was a police officer. I rang the doorbell, leaning forward on the doorpost, holding my thumping chest, trying to catch my breath, hoping I had not been spotted. Mr Brand answered. "Ahh, hello young lady, what can I do for you this evening? Sarah is in her room." He stood there with one bushy eyebrow raised, and both arms folded; he was very tall and authoritative.

"Mr Brand, you are a policeman, are you not?" I was just checking he had not retired. I had not seen him in a while, due to my sanctions and restrictions in seeing any other human life outside school hours. "Yes, I am Claire, why?"

"Well, do you have the authority to arrest both my parents for child cruelty, and take me into care tonight, please? I cannot stand it there a single second longer, and I do not have any money to place an advert in Nursery World to ask for suitable foster parents. Could you foster me, Mr Brand, please? Or how about adopting me? I'll work hard!"

"Oh well, it is not that simple. For starters, I do not go back to work until the morning, the police station is closed for now. You better come in, my love." He said this with a kind, calm and yet crafty voice, obviously making mental statements, just in case this ever goes to court. I prayed to the Gods of Justice in the Hague that it would. Before the nine o'clock news came on television, and before the sun had finally settled into the neighbouring land of Nottingham, Mr Brand hummed a song as he drove me home. My escape mission had failed. Social services were informed, but nothing happened after this episode; no Mrs Belvoir, no referrals, no adoption, no one came knocking at our bolted front door to save me.

After a long, tiresome April evening, Arthur had devoured his final whiskey for the night, then started another fight with me. I ate half my dinner before running from the table upstairs to my room to escape his verbal torrents. This time he followed me up the stairs, and all hell broke loose. He had unknowingly just stepped across the line into a new level of soul searching, as he was about to use up all his newly acquired enlightened twilight energy, by raging against the natural flow and order of my teenage existence. His midlife phase of rumination was well and truly over, as he showed no respect for my bedroom space, and the little treasured possessions I had, or for me, his flesh and blood. Arthur grabbed both my arms, shaking me into submission. He slapped my face many times, hitting my back when I turned away. His punches were so hard I fell to the floor. His rage was driven by his own frustrated adult life, so much so that his nostrils flared like a bull spooked by his own red mist. Then it happened, he spotted the one and only item of mine that brought me joy. He grabbed my cassette recorder and smashed it into tiny non-repairable pieces. Arthur took a deep breath in, dangling before me the set of special master keys which unlocked my bedroom window, and all other escape routes in the house. He grabbed all the pieces of my life together in his slender, manicured hands and threw everything out of the double-glazed window. As a million fragments of sound and metal hit the prized paving below, he ordered Rita to clean it up. He knew this hurt me more than his punches and insults.

My mother was becoming fearful that her housekeeping and additional wages would stop at any time if she showed any sympathy for me. She began to tear down my prized pieces of artwork and the few limited-edition Adam Ant posters, which I had spent an age collecting from the pile of mouldy recycled magazines at the Spiritualist Church. Rita snapped every single colouring pencil in two, between them, they took away everything that meant anything to me, including my dignity.

During that disturbed night, trying to close my sore and throbbing eyes for a few minutes, my spirit guide regulators called me in for an emergency sleep time meeting. They gave clear instructions and new coordinates. It was time to be a fearless young woman, and listen to what the next steps in this complicated process would be. Evolving faster than expected, I had reached my first major junction. I had already lost my dad to modern music and my mother to her new age translations, as she stayed anchored within the realms of kitchen Ouija and Grantham faith healing circles. There was no stopping me, as I astral travelled during sleep time some 5.878625 trillion miles from my bed in Grantham middle England, to far-flung orbits where Gene Roddenberry, George Lucas and Arthur C. Clarke went before me. I finally found refuge. It was 1982, I had no life skills to speak of, apart from mixing primary colours into secondary colours, and making music tapes with decorative sleeves. I knew I was still too young and inexperienced to be taken seriously; due to being a fifteen-year-old kid.

The early April morning brought dark skies and torrential rain. Arthur had skipped his twilight hot water and lemon, along with his sun salutations. Slamming the back door behind him, just to make his point clear, he went to his office earlier than usual. My bottom lip quivered, as my chest held tight its fear for my future. I watched him through the bars of the first-floor landing window, as he hurried to his car with slumped shoulders, now awkwardly drenched down to his cotton vest. He looked up at me, his eyes fixed on mine as he opened his car door, I was dead to him. He had made me. For this reason alone, he will continue to live on in my memory, encapsulated within the single rogue tear that trailed down my face, finding its own way to freedom as it hit the windowsill below. My creator took one last look up at me, our egos locked, as lifetimes of shared karmic pain linked us once again. There was something in the way he nettled a middle finger, that one gesture unchained us both.

Placing one foot in front of the other, navigating muddled emotions like a cognitive ninja dissident, alone and worried, I walked as I usually did to school. My entire body hurt, inside and out. Instead of attending registration, I went to the medical room and saw the school nurse. I sat down and cried in front of her. "What's the matter, Claire? What has happened?" She subtly observed the swollen blackening eye and reddened neckline. "I cannot go back home tonight," I sobbed. "My goodness me, when did this happen, who did this to you?" She was writing things down, noting the time on the wall clock above her desk, scanning my entire demeanour for anything further untoward. "Last night, in fact every night, they lock me in after school, on weekends and holiday times. The doors and windows have bars on them with special keys, the top row of kitchen cupboards have bells on them." "Bells! What do you mean, Claire?" A perplexed expression mounted her face, I would have done the same if I had heard all this for the first time. "Bells, alarms, they keep food in there and money," I whispered, as my throat was catching up with this latest soap opera episode, and was all ready to give me another bacterial infection. This time I was not silenced but listened to.

"Why would they keep food in there, Claire?" An excellent question, as we lived in modern-day middle England with fully stocked supermarkets. My dad had rolls of cash in his trouser pockets, he owned a factory, and our four-bedroom detached house with front and back gardens. He had a brand-new car bi-yearly, plus he bought Rita a vehicle of her own, (with which during her first weeks on the road, she managed to run over and kill Susie, our pet cat, which none of us ever forgave her for). So yes, why would my parents lock food in a cupboard? "Dad picks fights with me every dinner time; this left me feeling starved most nights." This was the truth. "Oh, dear me, you poor love, I need to check you over. Is this OK? I will have to see Mrs Belvoir, who may need to speak to your parents." She was kind and thorough. She found bruising along my arms, and the side of my face had a big angry slap mark that was still settling in, she wrote everything down in scribbly doctor's writing. "Yes, OK, can we all speak together maybe." I cried, as both eyes glazed over like a honeyed gammon, straight from the oven. Maybe now I can be adopted.

During the late afternoon period at school, sitting at the back of the home economics class, I tried to keep my cool. My colliding, retrograding, Aquarian astrological planetary predictions in the newspaper were not favourable at all. Aggressively, I beat too much air into the Victoria sponge batter, in hope of releasing some inner stress. Miraculously, twenty minutes later, it had risen beautifully, with the right amount of electric heat from the oven. Just as my intestines twisted like a Nordic pretzel, I wondered what the school nurse would say to my parents, but more worryingly, what would my parents say to her? The fire door flung open.

A group of men entered, wearing dull low-budget grey suits, standing in alignment to the pantry with Mrs Belvoir by their side. I dearly hoped they were from the Pentagon, searching for me. Mrs Belvoir looked mighty stern, her face never moved nor did a single hair on her head, only her frown line became a prominent gully of concern. She wore an expensive, fashionable, eighties trouser suit with sharp shoulder pads, as she stood tall and meant business, alongside the men. With the utmost discretion, the nervous home economics teacher kindly asked me to step out of the room. I reminded myself this was Grantham, not Washington DC, and making a getaway would never be discreet, especially since I was taller than my entire class. I tried to hold myself steady, but I looked more like an imbalanced NASA employee on the international space station. I felt like I was bouncing around in the atmosphere of classroom gossip, as whispers could be heard coming from behind flat floured hands. Mrs Belvoir went to discuss what happened with Mr Hull, who was very concerned. He never gave up on me, continuing to support all I did for many years to come.

Months into being a fifteen-year-old, I felt this life was taking an eternity to get going, but suddenly things were moving forward at a much faster pace. I found myself sitting in the passenger seat of a strange man's diamond blue Ford Cortina. Here I was, with one of the 'grey suits', who first asked me to put the seat belt on or his insurance would not cover me in the event of an accident. He smelt of ashtrays, and his suit jacket and miss-matched slacks were 100% poly casual, possibly the budget end of C&A. I made a mental note to myself, due to my ongoing obsessive observations of the way people dressed, concerning their authority.

"Hi Claire, please try not to worry, my name is Jones, and I am a social worker. Your mother did not want to talk to us at first." He said this as he fiddled with his seatbelt. I did not understand what he had just said, as I could not hear him due to the awful rattling and whirring noises coming from underneath the car. "YOU WHAT?" I yelled.

"I mean, well, your mother was far from a talking mood." He clarified that Rita was in one of her moods. "What about my dad?" Surely, he had something to say about this. I am his firstborn unless he had secret kids on the other side of the world with wife number one. "We tried to contact him, but we cannot get hold of him." "Hold on, is he a fugitive, has he been arrested?" I felt upset, as this sounded messy. I strapped myself tightly into his front seat. "No, he has not been arrested." "Did you ring his office yourself? I have the number in my head. I memorised it in case of emergencies. I think this is an emergency!" "Yes, it is an emergency," he agreed, as we started to drive away from the town centre. "Do you want his number, or shall we go around to the factory? He is not home until five-thirty-two, it is only three-thirty-one. I know the way, it's the next left at the traffic lights."

"No, we cannot go around there now, Claire. Your mother has signed a temporary order paper. This means that you are being received into care under section 2 of the 1980 Child Care Act. We will try to work this out; as this is only a short-term order, so you are going to stay with a family just outside Grantham. They are a nice couple with a small child." Section 2 of the 1980 Child Care Act is for when both parents orphan or abandon their child, which was me. Obviously, both my parents were in on this, and this social worker had just lied. I was seriously going to live with another family in a rural village, twenty-five miles away. Just as I collected my thoughts, we promptly arrived at a three-bedroomed bungalow, which had no upstairs. The noisy vehicle came to a crunching halt, as Jones miss-judged the breaks on the shingle driveway, so we both jolted forwards. On this rare occasion, I had to give thanks to the God of driving that we were strapped in.

A smiling couple came out to greet us. The foster folk were nervous, but as promised, welcoming and kind. Sandy and David were shop owners and had just adopted their four-year-old, her name was Emma. I was to share a room with Emma and sleep on the top bunk bed. How was this right, a fifteen-year-old who has always had my own room, now sharing with a four-year-old? When shown to our shared bedroom, I sat with Emma on her bottom bunk. Desperately I searched through the one-and-only bag Rita had packed. There were old pants, and odd school socks which I did not wear anymore; she had deliberately packed for yesterday's nine-year-old me. There were a pair of flip flops, and spare brown school uniforms which had been rolled up tight to fill the suitcase corners. Her home-made clothes were now 'last life', the whole suitcase of clothes suddenly felt even more spurious to my very being. I wore my school uniform on a Saturday, in protest until they found me a clothing grant.

Rita did not pack any of my music tapes. Her dominating, left-brained logic explained to her, in Pidgin English, that because my cassette recorder had been destroyed the night before, I would not need them, nor did I deserve them anymore. Whereas, my right brain common sense needed to hear music more than ever, to keep myself as wholesome as I could during this challenging time! The suitcase had no pens or sketchbooks, nothing for my creative wellbeing. There was one mint coloured flannel, some sanitary towels that took the shape of hoagie bread rolls, a toothbrush good enough to clean inside a plug hole, and some green Palmolive soap encased within a marble-effect plastic holder. Overall, this was child cruelty and a total disaster. Sitting in a complete state of shock on the squeaky bottom bunk, looking at various Athena posters of cartoon characters on the walls, I could not believe that I had wished so hard for something as dramatic as being adopted. Which was happening right now! This was my first insight into how the power of thought and dream interpretation worked.

I cried like a real girl. Did my parents hate me this much? Jones mentioned that they would be appointing a new female social worker, as this was only going to be a short-term situation. I had been removed for my own protection. It made no difference, whether it was short or long-term, the point was I had been kidnapped. My childhood was not as bad as the other girls at my school. There were secret pregnancies, abortions, adoptions, drugs, smoking, drinking. All I did was stand up for the people I knew nothing about, some shoplifting here and there, and subsequent terrible lying about the shoplifting. What had I done that was so unforgivable? How can a mother hate her child that much, for my situation to happen? The fact is our parents, our families, have one job to do, which is to keep us safe and healthy until we can do this for ourselves. In so many cases, including mine, this did not happen. It did not matter if they had money or not, wealth does not buy the protection, security or the happiness of a child. Wealth alone can be the abuser.

I just wanted us all to talk, but there was no talk or compromise. I was once great news; this country had been elated that I was coming to Earth. I was their firstborn, so what happened? How did my once childless young mother, feeling so desperate, even suicidal for a baby of her own, to now her abandoning me like this? Leaving me a motherless-child, alone and separated from my mother? Maybe I was becoming too expensive to keep, like a pony when it grows into a horse. I needed a mother to mother me, and a father to father me, I needed both equally to show me how this tricky life business works.

As promised, I was assigned a female social worker; her name was Bailey. She visited often and was one of the only female adults that I began to trust at this point. Bailey did, indeed, acquire a clothing grant. We went out shopping and bought a Ra-Ra skirt, and jeans with white piping down the side seams, and some red suede pixie boots with Cuban heels, zip and tassels. Bailey also managed to stretch the budget to buy a new cassette recorder, with combined radio. I was in heaven. I played my C-90 tapes so much; you could hear the reverse side playing backwards at the same time. We met up regularly, and Bailey soon became very involved with my progress and development. I was not going to be fooled by anyone this time, as I noted to myself that this was part of her job description, but I was becoming very fond of her.

NINE

Built with blindness, built in sight
Turning darkness into light.

The long and the short of being fostered was, for many reasons, it did not work out. After four months, the loneliness turned into isolation. The foster people were lovely, but they had a smaller child to take care of, being a fifteen-year-old misplaced teen who needed a room of her own, with a bed that was more fitting to my size was necessary. Bailey could see my dismay, so suggested I stay at a residential children's home back in Grantham. Within a nanosecond, two bags had been stuffed with new clothing and all my treasured art equipment and music tapes. The car could not drive fast enough towards Grantham town centre and my new life. I was thrilled that I was about to share a home with twenty-six other abandoned, neglected misunderstood kids. The residence owned a minibus to take us many places, so we could have exciting life experiences. This bonus was the total opposite to how I had been brought up, and the inner traveller I had always wished to be, reclaimed my heart. Even better, the staff at this kids' home were mainly females, this gave me precious time to catch up with my yin-yang imbalance.

One of the female staff on duty sat with me as I painted inside a donated sketchbook. My mind's eye was rapidly sifting through all the new fashion designs I wanted to create, then wear. She suggested I think about what I wanted to do when I left school, emphasising it was essential I be happy in the many years to come. If I was passionate about something, then I should go down those paths, like fashion. This was the opposite advice I had received from my company director father. For example, she loved children but was unable to have any of her own, so her career choice was perfect working in a home for kids. I thought back to my dad's misery; he should have been a musician, let my mum go out and earn money and to hell with the bills. We would have managed. Apart from my insular world of art and fashion, which could only ever be a hobby, so my dad kept drumming into me, my second love was music, so I got to work writing letters to companies where I could earn a decent living and paint in my spare time. EMI and CBS records came to mind, I asked for advice on getting a job with them in London, feeling a new kind of comfortable, with the prospect of a real job back in the city where I was born. My list of positive points was:

A) I loved art and music, I knew all the words of Adam Ants back catalogue, note for note, word for word, and had a secret liking for jazz.

B) I made perfect cups of tea with and without sugar, my coffee was not bad either.

C) I always had a tidy bedroom and could remember many things at the same time without having to write them down. I knew how an electric typewriter worked and would make a great secretary.

The reply from Miss Sullivan, the secretary, informed me that EMI was a professional record company, and they were not in the habit of employing children directly from the schools. They now required qualifications like a diploma or city of guilds of some kind, before they could take me on. It appeared I was still working on developing some further appropriate music industry skills since I had one more year of schooling to go. Miss Sullivan apologised if her reply was a tad disheartening, but explained that the music industry was very competitive, so she hoped the information she had given me was of help. CBS sent a similar, crushing letter. My music industry career was over before it had begun, so it was back to the drawing board for me. There was no way I could be a fashion designer because there would be too much drawing involved and drawing does not pay the bills.

Back at the residence, pocket money was issued every Saturday. I had never had pocket money before now. The amount depended on our ages, but the most significant privilege was to be able to have a Saturday job at my friend Joanne's pub. I made lunches and washed the dishes then managed to save all my wages in a savings account, until I had accumulated £50. I then bought a second-hand Techniques sound system, which included an excellent pair of Wharfedale speakers thrown into the deal. Carefully spacing both speakers for perfectly balanced sound, I imagined Arthur being proud of my choice. I also developed a keen passion for punk rock and new age electronic music. I was grateful it had gotten me through some of the most frustrating and heart-breaking junctures to date.

Surprising myself, I passed CSE art with an unexpected grade one, excelling in O-level art, earning an impressive Grade A, all thanks to the immeasurable support and complete dedication from my form and art teacher Mr Hull. I decided to go for my first dream, so applied to Lincoln College of Art and Design, the two-year Diploma fashion course, and was accepted! This was big news to everyone involved in my personal development and mental health. At sixteen, I felt all grown up and ready to leave the care system that had served me well. I had not ended up on the streets, on drugs, pregnant or on the dole, this surely was an achievement.

There must have been fifteen staff, teachers, assistants, and complete strangers sitting in one big circle, having a meeting about me in the common room. They were discussing whether they thought I had any talent at all, in anything, even though most of those present did not know me. With my nose pressed up against the glass of the enforced fire door, I could see them as they pretended not to see my pleading face. They passed around examples of my art work. Nodded in unison one minute, shaking heads the next. Eating their way through supermarket biscuits, hysterically laughing at something funny, picking noses, and yawning. Finally, all present were unanimously in favour that I was to attend Lincoln College of Art and be a full-time art student.

Bailey found a comfortable, fully-vetted, ground floor bedsit for me, with a nice back yard, for fifteen pounds a week. She explained that I needed to hold tight a bit longer, as I was still legally under social services care until I was eighteen. After being adopted, which happened in a temporary child care order kind-of-way, becoming an art student at Lincoln College had to be my next biggest dream come true, proving that thinking big, really got results.

Strangely, like Rita, I began making all my own clothes, first drawing, then cutting patterns from my own designs. I went to gigs every week and never took a day off college. Eventually, I obtained a Higher National Diploma merits in fashion and textile design. Sadly, neither of my parents attended nor acknowledged my final shows, when the people who made you do not care, failure is not an option. Meanwhile, Bailey and Mr Hull had travelled up to the North-East and had front row seats. How I loved these two people.

Four years after leaving school, now aged twenty, there was still no contact with my family. Alone and owing nothing financial to anyone, thanks to the bar work I did every evening and at weekends to supplement the small college grant I received from the government at the time, I relocated to Central London.

Before the computer age had reached the masses, the only way I communicated was by writing, by hand, grammatically incorrect letters to every London-based magazine, begging for a job doing anything in fashion. Kim was the new fashion editor at Blitz magazine, she replied. Kim was like no other woman I had ever known; her life energy created its own orbits. She was one of the original trendsetters, responsible for all the new romantic looks I had grown up with and greatly admired. I was scheduled to meet her at the very moment that fit perfectly into my cosmic timeline. According to my Earthland contract, one of the conditions in my life was not to jump stages and hurry time. I just needed to make it to the right place, which was here, at the right time, which was now.

My career highlights include; dressing the Oasis brothers the day before Princess Diana's funeral, (this was a very surreal day). Making authentic-looking angel wings for Bonnie Tyler and ironing Bryan Ferry's Yoji Yamamoto trousers. I had to sit still for over an hour, in a Parisian designer boutique, opposite a frantic Grace Jones, who was standing not three feet away from me, naked, while having a complete meltdown. I enthusiastically worked for Kim on most of the great artists of that time, including Janet Jackson, Boy George and the late, great George Michael, (when, during a particular fitting at his West London home, I unceremoniously fell down his carpeted stairs, landing on his beloved Labrador who was, luckily not harmed).

My most memorable job was the styling of Kylie Minogue in 1988. I had no clue who she was when my agent gave me the call. The assignment was to dress her for her first photo session as a solo artist, after Neighbours, the Australian soap opera. Kylie's record label, PWL, had briefed me that she was sixteen years old. I was to come up with a new image, to help her look like a funky, yet sophisticated twenty-year-old. I believed that I had done an excellent job since the pictures, which included her album cover, went global. My worst fashion nightmare unfolded just a few years later when those same highly-acclaimed photographs were publicly panned by the likes of Vogue and Elle fashion directors. They had gotten their Gucci talons into her, so 'lynch that stylist, whoever she was,' was shouted round popular Soho private drinking clubs and editorial haunts. Unfortunately, 'that stylist' was me! At the time, my pictures reflected her style of music, which was cheaply manufactured, eighties pop. But later, some smart producers created a new, more acceptably evolved, iconic inspiring, mainstream, dance-oriented music which looked to draw in the styling elite.

From 1991 to 2005, my full name suffered ostracism within the pop/media/clubland circuits, as I was that awful stylist who dared to dress the newly-crowned Queen of Pop in that (sold-out) Pam Hogg, classic red jersey dress and those iconic Red or Dead stack shoes, (which oddly sold over a quarter of a million pairs) thanks to those awful photos. Fast forward to 2005, when Kylie unfortunately, developed breast cancer, revealing she was, in fact, born in 1968. This baffled me, as 1968 was a year after I was born. Going back to that time in the photographic studio, she was a twenty-year-old, pretending to be a sixteen-year-old, wanting to look like a funky twenty-year-old. The mind boggles! The upshot was, in various coffee table books, there is a celebration of her successful second and third decade as

Queen of Pop. She was crowned the original eighties pop icon, thanks to that stylist back in 1988, namely me, who was not named publicly, until now!

Unexpectedly, my parents sent a 22nd birthday card. They had seen me appear on TV as a stylist a couple of times. Arthur had recorded it all on modern scotch videotape. Seven years on, both parents were still as alien to me as I was to them. My dad had completely lost his sense of humour, and nearly all his height and hair. His teeth were all there, but he looked old. I plucked up the courage to visit them some months after receiving the card, both were still notably dismissive of everything I tried to share, explain, discuss, or debate with them. The exciting seven years of fun tales, of being the real Claire, fell on deaf ears. I had gained life experiences that were not the same as theirs because it was my life, which they did not like nor even wish to understand.

During the next few months, my relationship with all my family became strained. I grew in experience and confidence; through the great work, I was being paid handsomely to do. I was a creative, healthy, happier person with no throat illnesses. Yet they clearly resented my success, not pleased with any of my triumphs, picking at threads wherever the stitching was just nearing perfect. They continued to make sarcastic comments about most things, yet it was my craft and sharp eye in design that paid my bills. Rita thought I dressed strangely, but I was just my true independent self. On one visit to Grantham, my contribution to Sunday dinner was broccoli, and mange tout, bought from Berwick Street Market in Soho. Rita's face looked as if I had given her raw kryptonite to boil and she was Clarke Kent's mother, not mine. The London organic superfoods turned into tasteless soup. The KX-T5101C answer phone I had bought for Dad for Christmas was a different story. It was a real winner, as he loved new gadgets. Dad, still the company director, kept phoning himself from work to leave a voice message to playback when he got home. Unfortunately, Rita kept answering the phone as she was his home-based secretary, doing her bit for womankind.

As might be expected, my biological mother yet again chiselled another chink into my fast-deflated aura, by typing a badly-spelt letter, addressed to me in King's Cross London, explaining that they had all had enough of my adult city ways, they preferred I stay away. I felt cheated that this life-of-Claire was now to be led, family-less. My working life was doing great, my emotional life was the opposite. I crashed headfirst into a nebulous depression that lasted three long, painful months. If this was really my film, surely the principal actor had a right to quit the stage, in her final dramatic scene.

Weeks went by, the curtains were permanently drawn. I went from a well-paid fashion stylist to withdrawing into wearing frumpy unlabelled jogging bottoms and plain t-shirts. My teeth began to decay with neglect. I would not leave my Kings Cross flat until the hour of darkness high fived my moods. Head lowered, fists clenched, I strolled over to the corner shop on the Kings Cross Road in my pyjamas, wearing fake Ray-Ban sunglasses and thinking nothing of the fact that I looked like a central London junkie. On ambitious days, I dressed around two in the afternoon after watching every minute of *This Morning* with Richard and Judy. Religiously I dialled their daily phone-in cash competition, using my red BT *Viscount* push-button home phone, as no one earning under £100,000 had a mobile phone back then. Wandering around in central London, looking for any kind of inspiration to kick start the next part of my evolution, a decorative notebook and fountain pen became my friend. It held most of my top-secret fashion predictions and emergency phone numbers, doodle sketches, designs, ideas, notes, verses, and words that balanced material wants against spiritual leanings. At least that part of me had not died. My active mind continued to spark ideas and make plans; which meant I was just heart dead, as I contemplated that I had been created by two people who did not want me as a child, and nor now as an adult either.

My savings earned from 'drawing pictures' were dwindling. They barely stretched to pay phone bills, thanks to Richard and Judy's competition phone-ins, and the accumulating countless self-help spiritual books, which were all the new-age rage of the time. This Eighties mystical stuff could be practised anywhere, at any time. The words on each page became my new drug of choice, becoming addicted to modern-day guru mantras and peppermint tea, the winds of change blew active and energetic within my little London bedsit. This universe had entered a new, more cosmic era, one of finding self-acceptance and answers to profound psychological questions, even generational behavioural explanations which emerged, through books, seminars, and retreats. Unfortunately for me, I was born out of the womb of the depressive post-war generation. Since birth, I had dragged myself through the muddy trenches of life, finally reaching the friendly territories of 1989.

During this time of self-imposed convalescence, I refrained from drinking alcohol or taking the prescription drugs urged on me by my concerned doctor. I needed to feel every part of my pain, not dumb it down further, by monitoring its depth so I could, if I chose to, crawl out of it at any time. This was the time when I met my neighbour, Michael, who was twenty years my senior and an engaging writer, who inspired me greatly. He used to knock on my door to make sure I had a hot meal inside me, as he listened to my triumphs and woes. Secretly, he was collecting inspiration himself, for characters for his next scripts and scenes.

This time was my first memory of a spiritual awakening, after shutting myself down as a kid, primarily because of all those spooky gifts I possessed. Now, more than any other time in all my combined lives, I needed to open that locked box of tricks back up again. Avidly, I read anything Deepak, Jung, Freud, even Montessori and Steiner to see where my parents had gone wrong. I put myself out on a limb, journeying the road less travelled, working out how many lives and masters I had, and still had to endure. Making my own Celestine Prophesies, as I had walked through this life fearless from birth, I began to feel the fear; I did it anyway all while trying to be a peaceful urban warrior.

Trapped within the desolation of darkness called depression, I politely prayed to God, Buddha, or Elvis, to please end my suffering. Finally, reality struck, three months was enough time spent being miserable, slumping around in oversized men's pyjamas. The phone bill was getting out-of-hand, as I had not won a thing on morning television competitions, so I needed to get back to work. It was the beginning of summer, the most perfect time to spring clean away my entire family and life, and accept they were not deserving of this level of misery from me. I was worth a lot more. That night, I went to sleep in sobbing tears. Waking early, I felt oddly super, as if all the badness had been sucked out of me using a happiness dialysis.

Maybe this was it, I had to learn to understand that I was not going to have any loving, kind, biological parental assistance from today onwards. I needed a competent defence team to help fight these tiresome battles. Then again, if I thought about it, I had no parental support thus far in life, so I was no worse off. My friends were becoming my only family, and I was learning to love them for all the different and beautiful things each one of them did in their lives and did for me. The landline rang, it was not the official ITV competition people, it was a friend inviting me out to a nightclub in West London that evening.

Riding high on the night winds of early nineties techno sounds, under oscillating disco moonbeams, dropping something on the dance floor, my eyes met Ben. He was five years older than me, exceptional at folding clothes, and computer coding. He taught me how to create home-cooked meals from scratch, and how to display edible food, like oil on canvas or clay on a wheel, well before the likes of TV super cooks. Our relationship blossomed over the next couple of years. Sometime during 1992, Ben insisted on teaching me how to use a computer, for he was a marvel at anything technical. A bizarre request, since I had no previous desire to own a computer. I was not a magazine editor or journalist of any kind; I could barely spell my own name. Oddly, computer lessons in the early nineties turned into one of my greatest achievements, I was trained and digitally armed for the 21st Century. This was a time when only a few people knew what a home computer or electronic mail account was. I learnt fast and had gained valuable new-age skills, apart from Ben, there was no one to email until at least 1996.

My other grand achievement during this great romance was learning how to drive a car. This turned out to be not just any old relationship. No one had ever invested this much time and energy into assisting me with all these valuable life skills. By 1993 I owned a BMW 320I, and an Apple Macintosh home computer, I had never been so grown up.

My styling agent had bookings for me all over London, with all sorts of weird and wonderful jobs. Ben and I moved into our new flat in North London. This was the first time I had committed myself so deeply to one person. We travelled continuously all over Europe and America, as Ben had many work connections almost everywhere on the planet. This was, by far, an exciting time. At night we went dancing till dawn, or occasionally until lunchtime the next day, in many secret London underground clubs. In the day time, I composed myself as best I could, while dressing music artists and bands for video, editorial, and advertising shoots.

One lazy Saturday morning, Ben laid on the sofa in the living room watching match of the day highlights. I was feeling very unwell, struck by a dull, crippling pain that shot down both legs. I ran to the toilet to be sick, collapsing on the windowless basement bathroom floor with a thud. No one could hear me, as the loud extractor fan was busy whirring recycled air above my head. My body was wedged up against the radiator, which was on full heat. Unable to move a muscle, with no audible voice coming from my mouth, what do I do now? Ben eventually came in, he found me in a sweating heap on a top of a black shaggy bath mat on the floor. I was bleeding heavily. As at this point there was minimal response from me, he promptly called 999 on the newer BT '*Statesman*' landline phone. The ambulance crew arrived, took one look at the job ahead and commented under their breaths that I was a heavy one, not realising I could hear every word. I was five-foot-eleven, a half-conscious dead weight with no underwear on at all, in a basement flat which posed a kinetic lifting problem to their stocky frames. They kindly moved me away from the radiator before I developed third-degree burns in my upper shoulder, while they considered calling for back-up to lift me. My pallor did not look right, they checked what was in the toilet, assessed the blood loss on the black rug, measuring the clots seen sticking to the fibres. Swiftly they swaddled me inside a red blanket and strapped me tight on to a carry chair.

Once onboard the ambulance, the beeps of the ECG monitor sounded like a frantic game of Atari Pong, which took me back to playing this with my dad. Where was my dad? Questions bounced around between the paramedic and Ben, then. "Pulse 42, BP 85/50, shit mate, put the lights on," said the concerned paramedic, just before my hearing went. My last thought was, how cool his job was, just before my imaginary film crew could get the shot of this man jumping up and down on my chest, saving my life. I woke up at the Royal Free North London in resuscitation one. "How are you, Claire?" Ben asked as he put my hand into his hand. "Look, I have some news, the doctors said it looks as if you miscarried."

"Pregnant?" My heart sank, I felt so stupid, because I had no idea.

Something so powerful had died that day. Sadly, my faith in Ben had all but disappeared too. At twenty-nine years of age, I had lost a long-term relationship, a ton of blood, and a foetus. At no time during the past seven years had we ever talked about starting a family of our own, as we were too busy having a good time. This had me worrying that there was something deeply wrong with me as a woman, I had become the exact opposite to my own mother, now being too feminist and free and not very maternal. Another vivid night dream explained where I was to go next. I left London shortly after, to travel to Nepal alone.

TEN

You are back beyond the blue my friend
Beyond the blue, and drowning.

My thirty-year-old self knew that this should have been the right time to start a family, but instead, I travelled for months through India and Nepal, which gave me time to think and explore myself, as well as that part of the world. Enrolling into meditation and yoga classes, I realised that my mounting fear of parenthood boiled down to dread that I, too, would end up a horrible mother just like mine own. However, since the miscarriage, my new fears were of not being able to carry a baby to full term, and of childbirth itself, things I had given little thought to before the loss. It hit me hard, feeling that I had not been responsible enough to keep a baby-safe, nor in tune with my body's rhythms to know I was carrying a child in the first place. I was a mind person, and always lost in thought, some people said I lived there. The previous weeks to the miscarriage, I felt nothing trimestral, apart from being highly emotional, while acting a little bit spiteful.

This event changed my direction. I had grown up within a family of emotive hibernators. Our shared surname forbade any of us to explore or express our feelings on any subject, for fear of matriarchal reprimand. I had not learnt how to articulate my feelings; hence I left my relationships when things got bad because I had witnessed how bad things got when two people stayed together under duress. Being asexual, to a degree, during my most fertile childbearing years was a kinder option than considering raising another messed-up family.

The practical part of my spiritual journey began that day I lost a baby. While in India, I received many mindful images and visions of my spirit guide during meditations and sacred readings, this was comforting and confirmed that I am never alone. It was suggested that things had to change. To Keep Watch began spitting feathers, eyebrows crossed, imploring I start this part of my life plan sometime soon. At thirty-one and alone, I returned to South-East Asia, travelling through India from Delhi onto Bombay, then Goa. A second-class, windowless, sleeper train's top bunk became my temporary home. Swiftly travelling the circuit onwards to calmer tranquil Kerala, I landed in Varkala where I rented a shack. It was the most basic, bare-bones of backpacking accommodation, with a few bamboo leaves for a roof and some mud slapped on the walls for structure, but by now, wherever I laid my backpack was home. Perched upon the top of the south-facing cliff, the sunshine drained away any energy I had on reserve as the tropical heat was inescapable. Fortunately, there was at rare times a slight breeze, which made up for the lack of any air conditioning. There was no electricity, so no fan.

I usually have wintery birthdays, sometimes it even snows, but on this auspicious 33rd Indian February birthday, thin humid air tried to crush both of my struggling lungs. While I strolled along the sandy beaches, there were a couple of official men standing over a dead, six-foot-five, waxy white male surfer, the first fallen human I had ever seen. It seemed to take the Indian authorities a couple of hours to think of what to do next. The crowd was multiplying, ground heat intensifying when they decided to carry him on a makeshift stretcher made of two bamboo poles that had been tied to a single batik sarong. Six men were wading through the deep hot sand, with many curious onlookers close by. They loaded him into their ten-foot Rascal ambulance, but this did not leave much room up front to drive safely. Horrified, I watched as they grabbed a long pole with a brick strapped to it, which became a makeshift hammer, they took a big swing and smashed both his legs. The growing audience all winced, some looked away, while many locals took sneaky snaps for their macabre tourist albums. Hurriedly, placing him in the back of this tiny vehicle, with his legs broken, they were able to shut the single back door safely so he would not fall out. His wrinkled bare flesh was ghostly and translucent, noticeable because both feet were wedged firmly against the slightly tinted back window, which was covered in surfing stickers.

Later that same afternoon, the humidity had reached a staggering eighty per cent. Everyone that needed to paddle in the sea, sneakily urinated out any hydration left. I stood with both knees bent in the water so that it came a little over my shoulder height. Someone screamed out a warning and turning around quickly, I was met by an angry wave. Before logic could tell my body to duck under the water, it smacked the side of my face with such an almighty clap, it caused my neck to crick. With no time to take a breath, its force pulled me under into its effervescence. Disorientation panicked me, as the bubbles confused which direction to swim for air. The strength of water dragged me downwards, where it felt for a moment comfortably cooler. The little breath remaining evaporated, darkness was all around. My mouth began to open, surrendering the life I had just lived. This felt like the right and only thing to do. Someone grabbed hold of my neck, pulling me up through the warmer waves and into the brightest sunlight. A stranger had reacted so fast, impulsively saving my life.

Earlier that same birthday, a random stranger had died. I wondered, if I had been there when he was in trouble, would I have braved the sea or even known what to do? How can my Fashion Diplomas and impressive media phone list be of any use to me? I felt total frustration because someone was there for me; just in time! A hero had saved my life on the same day the surfer died. Why had I been saved? I watched the sun setting while I sat on a rock by the beach, and I thought long and hard about where my life was heading.

It was now 2000, the dawn of a new Millennium. Once the white, cracked soles of my feet had landed back on British tarmac, my need to withdraw from modern life became overwhelming. The chaos of India had changed me. My spirit had become used to an exciting Indian existence, calmer and not-so-fiery curries, basic materialism, strange encounters, incredible views, and fascinating people. My needs now were to read more soul-searching books, to watch daytime television, to enter more give-away phone-in competitions, but this time, by using my one new joy, the first-ever Motorola Graphite-flare mobile phone.

Six weeks passed, and since I had not won any competitions, money was tight. Walking into Kentish Town one afternoon, I noticed a job advertised in the jobcentre window. It said London Ambulance were recruiting technicians. I did not have a clue what that was, but it sounded exciting. Coincidentally, at that same moment, a yellow Mercedes ambulance drove past with its sirens and lights on. I went right in and applied. Thinking back to the miscarriage, hearing the paramedics in the ambulance, overdosing aged fourteen, it was all connecting. Suddenly gratitude towards Ben, for enabling me to get my driver's license and be computer savvy ignited within me. My world became easier to navigate with a car and a mouse. I silently thanked everyone for all the life skills I had learnt over the years since leaving home. Immense gratitude to the person I witnessed dead in India; and to the person who saved me, for without them, I would never have questioned anything to do with saving a life. Something clicked, giving a rare moment of third eye alchemy. Everything I had suffered, from birth to now, had been part of my unique divine plan. I was meant to lose that first baby. All those far away countries I had travelled were the conduit to the next chapter, the next decade of my life. Slowly, but surely, I learnt how to read all those subtle connections and unavoidable disasters. I acknowledged the reasons behind every tragedy I experienced, we were all connected.

Joining London Ambulance Service was an incredibly proud moment; no one in my family had done anything like this before. The interview went well because they were impressed with all my worldly travels, and my previous career choice as a fashion stylist. To the interviewing panel, this proved I understood diverse situations, with people from varied cultural backgrounds, showing I could work under pressure. The training course proved very difficult for me, as my English and maths had never been up to professional standards. Medical words went straight through my head unless I was shown a photograph or illustration. My passing out ceremony was a proud moment, where my new Earth parents, Brenda and Michael, my friend from King's Cross, came to enjoy the day. Both were becoming the parents I missed having. Once I passed the initial training, I was monitored for the first year on the road. During daily shifts, the strange stories of the people of London were presented to me, with many scenarios. Some were easy, others memorable, some logistically tricky, including impossibly heavy lifts within challenging locations, often with very ill individuals with multiple conditions. The first thing I knew, from experience, was not to voice my concerns within earshot, just in case the patient could still hear.

There were a few emergency jobs that immediately changed me from that moment onwards. My most memorable and horrific trauma jobs were, oddly, maternity jobs. It was only ten minutes till the end of my first ever night shift, at zero-six-fifty we got a call to go to a BBA (Born Before Arrival), it was an Indian woman. The baby was struggling to breathe because he was three months premature. The mother kept saying, "Baby is gone, bad soul, take it away, away, away." She shooed us all away. Having spent valuable time in India, I understood that she was Hindu. The Hindus firmly believe the baby has chosen not to come into that body, for whatever reasons, and the soul of that baby will go on to reincarnate somewhere else immediately. I imagined that the mother-to-be would feel rejected after carrying it for so long. When does the soul enter the body, and when does consciousness become conscious? Hindus believe that, from birth until the age of five, if a child dies his/her body, which has been made up of Dhara (Earth), Nabh (Ether), Vayu (Air), Varuna (Water), Agni (Fire) is buried. The body can then disintegrate back into the earth so not to be cremated. The belief is that the soul has not stayed in the body long enough to have any attachments to it, and parents can grieve their loss a little easier. This kind of situation was still very distressing to hear, especially while myself, my crewmate, and a first responder, were all trying to save the baby's life. A pointless task, if the soul has already moved on elsewhere.

Another ambulance crew had arrived, taking over the care of this hysterical mother who was fighting us. The combination of labour, along with the loss of her baby, was simply too much. This experience would stay with her indefinitely. I could not imagine the depths of her loss as I grabbed the lifeless body of her son with both hands; running down five flights of stairs keeping up with chest compressions with one finger and wisps of breath into his little, loose mouth. My crew mate drove towards St Mary's Paddington. In the end, the baby had died. Night shifts, working weekends and every single bank holiday frustrated the free-thinking, open-minded, inner traveller Claire. I had a punishing schedule, with no powers to change things around to suit myself.

A fifteen-year-old mother had just delivered, by herself, a seventeen-week old sleeping baby boy. He was born within the urine-soaked lift of her twenty-fourth floor West London council flat. As my crewmate and I arrived at the elevator, she was screaming her heart out, as she held her baby tight in her cupped hands, the umbilical cord was still attached. Desperately I looked for any signs of life, as there was no heartbeat inside this tiny, fragile body. His translucent lips matched his fingertips as he peacefully laid in her hands. With the help of my crewmate, we clamped, then cut the umbilical cord, and wrapped a red blanket around mum, who was uncontrollably trembling due to unbearable trauma. She was just a baby herself, who had had no idea she was pregnant in the first place. She thought she was having a painful period, which was part of her medical history. For her to deliver a baby by herself, then to see him lifeless in her hands in a stinking council lift, was not the dream any woman has. She clung on to him, kissing his face many times, saying she loved him over and over; she would have made a great mother. Hanging on to every word we said, she responded as best she could. With the utmost care, we explained what we were going to do for her. She nodded, with a longing for her sleeping baby deep within her eyes.

"Is he dead, am I going to die?" This is when you need your wits about you, as she will remember every word I say, just like I remembered every word that the London crew said when I miscarried in the bathroom. However, this bore no resemblance to that day at all. She held the tiny body of her son in her shaking hands. "Yes, your baby is dead, I am so sorry. But you, my love, will not die, not on my watch! Now let us get you, and your beautiful son, cleaned up and into the hospital. Let us think of some sweet names for him, shall we?" The placenta had not come, so we decided to make our way to the hospital quickly. While mum was laying down on our trolley bed in the back of the ambulance, I rolled blankets under her knees to assist with her posture and help ease her physical pain. I understood that no number of blankets, even if I shaped them into decorative birds, could ever heal this kind of pain. My crew mate checked her vitals one more time, as I laid my clipboard down, shuffling up next to her on the narrow trolley bed. Both of my arms wrapped around her slumped shoulders. Both her hands held onto her eternally sleeping baby son, his face was perfect, almost smiling at peace. It made no sense.

For eighteen months, I worked alone on the rapid response car around the congested roads of North-West London. On this particular day, strong seasonal winds had blown deciduous leaves from huge swaying trees above; each leaf left its mark, like a pathway, on the road in front. Control called me on the *Nokia 3310* works phone, not by radio as was usual, asking would I mind attending a stillbirth in progress? I hesitated, as I had participated in too many of these kinds of situations of late. Regardless of my mood, they sent me to do the job.

"Go ahead with details." I lowered my UV sunglasses from my head, placing them firmly on the bridge of my nose, flicking the lights and sirens on, driving at a reasonable speed on top of the Autumnal shedding of dead leaves that lined the road ahead. The thought of what was to come was unthinkable. As I approached, no one flagged me down. This generally happens, so I was temporarily lost within the maze of grey, pebble-dashed council flats. Outside the flat, I rang the bell and waited. To wait was also unusual for this kind of job, typically when there is a death, someone is usually flagging us down in the street. A solemn-looking gentleman opened the door; he was a relative within a large Somalian family. Inside, there were eight people, all standing around one struggling lady, who was sitting all by herself on the floor. Even though she was Somalian, her skin was ashen with hypotension, this was not a good sign. The baby's head was out, but there was no life force left in him or his mum. No one was helping her, not even to hold her hand; she sat at the foot of a tatty old armchair, not bothering to push.

I was on my own, apart from the voice of ambulance control coming from a Nokia 3310, telling me there were no crews available in the area. I checked the mother; she was hypotensive. I tried to encourage her to push, but the baby was stuck. He was obviously dead, so she was my only priority. I asked if someone could get us both some water, no one moved. I dropped to one knee, repositioning her lower back and legs. Teaching her how to suck on the Entonox mouthpiece I hoped this would help with any contractions, but she did not speak English, nor did she understand how to take in the gas and air from the mouthpiece. She inefficaciously blew instead. There were no screams, not a single sound came from her or anyone in the room. Silence surrounded this stillbirth.

After fifty minutes, still working alone, with one last push, the baby finally slid out into my hands. Immediately I rubbed him down while trying to revive him, checking his heart by attaching a three-lead ECG to his tiny chest for a full minute, alert for any signs of life, but there were none. He was a full-term baby boy, born at 40 weeks and 5 days. Wrapping him up in the towelling cloth, I asked if anyone could hold him while I checked where the placenta was, no response. With respect, I tried to lay him down on the sofa. The family would not allow me to do this. A tall thin man stepped forward and wagged his finger, giving me a frighteningly stern face of disapproval, then he said, "No bad baby on the chair." I asked the family to please work with me; they would not move, let alone help. I placed the baby down on the chair regardless of their beliefs; he was wrapped up tight, his face covered over with the lip of the towelling dressing. They were not happy, but I stood my ground. I oversaw this situation with authority, explaining that mum was in a critical condition. It took ninety minutes before a crew arrived. By that time, she still had not passed the placenta. Her pulse tachycardic, she was pyretic, dripping in perspiration, her raven skin became ashen with hypoxia.

The double paramedic female crew arrived, so we got her and her baby safely into the ambulance very quickly, and off they went to the hospital. I ran back to my works car. The alarm had been going the whole time. This had infuriated one of the neighbours, who had left a nasty note on my windscreen. Dumping all the medical bags on the pavement, I searched to find my keys. The neighbour promptly came out from his council flat, shouting the inconsiderate car alarm riot act. He did not care that it was an ambulance car, or that a baby had died almost next door. I was in bits. Momentarily remembering all the enlightenment training I had received in Asia. But right then, I struggled to remain Zen.

Two weeks later, a European articulated lorry smashed into the rear of my works car, shunting me to the other side of Shepherds Bush roundabout. This was when months, maybe years, perhaps even lifetimes of heartache poured out of me. All my planets collided; Mercury retrograded my destiny path into oblivion. That lorry bumped me right off that path of frontline work, into the unknown. I voluntarily left the service shortly after, all on good terms, alas, with a dint in my pride and a developing case of tinnitus.

I had hoped my role as Claire, the thirty-something, childless, adult professional, had been part of some stranger's solution. I prayed my positive presence had been the cavalry, so to speak, their help, healing, the answer, the successful onward story, the beginning of something wonderful, or a happy conclusion to something terrible. Maybe, to some strangers, I did make a difference. On the other side of the coin, the real me, the misunderstood abandoned child of Claire, now aged thirty-eight, still cried almost daily into a large white wine and supermarket-ready meal. The reality was, at the end of every shift, I came home to no one. Day after day, shift after shift, I hid behind an unflattering, man-sized green uniform while suffering from regular seasonal throat problems. I had hoped that this career in helping people would help me, and in many ways, it did. I had been part of some unbelievable life-changing events. I had certainly been enriched because of them.

My body then reached a point of complete shutdown, I had an official episode of post-traumatic stress, which was the new, fancy medical description for my dear old friend, depression. In 2006 during my thirty-ninth year, my life had become a train crash, hitting another decade junction, which was fast becoming a decennium habit. Without proper thought, I handed back the keys to my lovely London flat to go travelling the world, moving out on the day of my fortieth birthday, even going as far as to disconnect my *BlackBerry 6710*. Finally, I felt free of everything; so free, in fact, that I was officially contactless and homeless.

At this point in my life, I still blamed my parents. Although this current crisis was not their fault, where were they for the last forty years for support, a phone call, or a hug? As I gently cantered bareback into middle age, nothing much was working out for me anymore. I was fraught with the belief that no one truly loved nor championed me. I had great friends, plus Brenda and Michael who had somehow become parental stand-ins. I had partners who tried their best, but the fault lay at my feet, as I did not love myself. Writing this on paper was a challenge to read back, but it needed admitting to myself first. It became apparent that the love I desperately desired to feel, had to come from within.

ELEVEN

Blaze your bridges, then turn your page.

Booking a one-way ticket to Mexico City in early December 2006 did not seem crazy at all. However, leaving London in February 2007, to go travelling, with a twelve-inch laptop (with built-in Wi-Fi), a single sixty-litre backpack, and an MP3 player, only put my tummy in the worst headphone travel knot imaginable. With no London home anymore, no significant belongings (since I sold almost everything I ever owned) and no job to come back to, I had left myself open to all possibilities. I wondered if I would ever return to the old Claire.

My ever-trusted internal compass guided me to lay down my backpack in one of the most beautiful places in this world, Lake Atitlan in Guatemala. Stumbling across a health food shop in Panajachel, run by Linnet Kerr; her smile and warm greeting was the medicine I was seeking. It seemed as if we had known each other for many lifetimes, and she already felt part of my ongoing story. Linnet was a craniosacral therapist, a healing method that tunes into the flow that connect to the spinal cord, which ultimately joins the dots to everything universal. Our brain is lubricated and cushioned in a cerebral-spinal fluid. Surrounded by the Dural membrane lining of the inside of the skull and spine, it is in a constant state of perpetual rhythmic motion. Restrictions and blockages within the body can be felt at a cellular level and can be released by those blessed with gifted healing hands. Linnet had those hands, by palpating the rhythm with feather-lite fingers and by using her hauntingly beautiful intonations, she began to assist me.

One morning, the lake in Atitlan was the calmest and clearest it had been in days. Gently swaying in a big blue launcha taxi boat, my solar plexus was stuffed full of turbulence while on my way to my first session. Laying on Linnet's table, she sat behind me holding my head with her fingertips; as she would a new-born baby. She whispered nothing but sisterly kindness into the unloved soul I had been dragging around for the last forty years. She immediately felt my first dilemma surface. My left female had lost her magnetism, and the right male energies were overbearing, in fact, they were both frantically moving in every direction around my body avoiding each other. Her voice sounded like a thousand years of opera, all neatly rolled into one controlled breath. With her psychic eyes and fast hands, she pulled out invisible, unwanted emotional debris of past pain.

During a subsequent session, my body became pyrexical, as Linnet worked feverishly hard, heat accompanied prickly sensations under my skin. Swirls of old body clutter, stagnant buried emotions, rose to the surface, where vivid memories cried out to be freed from dated exhausted timelines. My male and female energies were in a historic battle. The male part had dreamt of playing a musical instrument, just to one day please Arthur, my jazz dad. Meanwhile, my female warrior cried out that she wanted to go clothes shopping with post-war Rita. There was no peace, both parties screeched offkey, ear-deafening sounds, that came from my voice box. After one further session, both polarities began clearly defining themselves as I cried out, coughing up unfiltered forgotten memories. My male began to harmonise, as he started to play the most exceptional clarinet solo of Aker Bilk's *Strangers on the Shore*, all in C major with no sharps and no flats. My female also finally felt contentment, as she draped herself in the most exquisite couture. I felt the connection more than ever before, as Linnet unmasked, layer by layer, the raw me. My inner cogs now held better time than Casio.

Somewhere between waxing crescent to waxing gibbous, Linnet walked me through six separate sessions of healing treatments, one for each of my six chakras. Each time something very different and powerful came up; I screamed, cried, laughed myself into tearful hysteria, then released it all with controlled breathing until I had nothing left to release. Linnet held me safe. Our final, seventh session took place at midnight under a full moon, floating in a natural hot springs tub. The natural water made my blood dizzy, imagining being back in the womb, the one I did not want to come out of in the first place. I saw my mother aged twenty-three, she was beautiful, wearing a Twiggy short haircut, but this time I let go of expectations, and rebirthed the forty-year-old cultivated Claire.

Moving on to Antigua, Guatemala, I came across a Shamanic teacher. Don José took one look at my Mayan birth chart, also known as Nawal, and told me my first sign is 12 Ba'atz. To be honest, I had no clue what he was saying. "My dear, you come to me on the most auspicious day for your development. I can see you are a threader-of-time, and a community host. You need to create community wherever you go. Aah yes, a true master of time. You see things coming, but you act on this information fast." He continued. "A natural midwife, 7-Kawooq, your life is about babies and children. You have children?" This was an unexpected and utterly crazy question, as I had spent my entire life avoiding such things, this could be the reason I had felt so lost, I am not on the right path. "No, José, but I have recently delivered many babies with my job." Within that one reflective sentence, pride leapt from deep in my heart up to my mouth. "You will be having babies of your own. It is never too late; you are here to guide others through your children." José continued explaining that I am truly blessed to have seventy-six shamanic spirits following me on my journey, (the highest is eighty-six) this meant I do not have a choice about being on a spiritual path. Whenever I go astray, the Universe will put me on the next bus back to spirit base camp.

José's unique course was an intriguing, twenty-one-day, Water Path Shamanic Training School. He would teach me how to open my third eye, to see clearly through dream states and into other ethereal realms. Twenty-one days of hard work would complete one full Mayan month, earning me the right to become a Mayan Shaman Priestess. I would then receive my Pixolkakal (pronounced pish-om-ka-kal), meaning, true Mayan authority and power. No animals or hallucinogenic drugs would be used for anything I was about to learn.

After completing this course, my Nawal conception, mission, spiritual power, material power, female and masculine DNA and transformation would align together. José demonstrated using dried red coffee beans and a lightweight paper grid drawn with red inks, that he had made himself from berries. It resembled a bingo card and showed how my inner potential suggested great universal work to come. The power of a female 12 Ba'atz could run for President, head parliaments, and run a small country. "José, as the Gregorian month is different from the Mayan, when is my Mayan birth date?" I enquired with a deeply inquisitive brow. "This will be the 10th of September 2007, in two weeks' time, this year you are 40 years old in Gregorian, but in Mayan you will turn 50!" He moved the coffee beans around the almost translucent paper chart, like a game of drafts. I was just about to ask. "And before you ask, this means dear child, in the end year of Maya 2012 when in Gregorian years you will be of 45 years of age, your Mayan age will be 55. I see great pain for you within that year. A unique baby will be born. This is when you will come into your full priestess power. You have lived here within the Mayan timeline before. Welcome home, my friend." I did feel at home in Guatemala but found that last comment, about a baby and me, very tough to believe. I did indeed work hard for every one of those twenty-one days, earning my new title of Mayan Water Path Shaman Priestess. My awareness fine-tuned, consciously shifting into other, crazy dimensions. The window between my eyebrows opened another degree, and that seventy-six strong angelic team were activated, ready to take on whatever was coming next.

After leaving South America, I flew to South-East Asia, taking my time continuing to cultivate my soul. While in Bali Indonesia, I attended a Balinese family cremation. The Balinese send their dead to the Nirvana realms with such a profoundly passionate show of honour, love, and creativity; it is a true celebration of life. I accepted a rare invitation to go into the family home, which was made up of many smaller apartments within one big courtyard. The main building in the centre of the courtyard, called the casabo, is where the women of the house give birth, then nurse the child for the first three months. The casabo is also used to rest their dead, while the village priest works out the best astrological time in their two-hundred-and-ten-day calendar year to cremate the bodies. This could be held the very next day or in some cases four, eight, or twenty years after death. When this happens, the body is buried in the ground then exhumed at the most auspicious time for cremation.

My heart sank when I realised it was a fifteen-year-old boy who had passed away. He had been killed in a motorbike accident three days before. All his school friends were present, and even though the Balinese way to cope with death is not to cry and mourn but to celebrate the life and be happy, it was hard to conceal such saddened emotion. Within Balinese Hinduism, also called 'Agama Tirtha,' the children who pass over, do not always reincarnate straight away. Their purpose is to be born to give the families deep soul meanings, or it is perceived as karmic payback or a soul lesson. When children die, they are rewarded eternally in Nirvana (Heaven) for completing this selfless journey.

The Gong Beri band softly played percussion music in the background; it was hardly noticeable, and yet my foot was lightly tapping to its enchanting beats. The friends of the boy sat in small groups, some in school uniforms, some in traditional Balinese sarongs. Holy water sprinkled like rain-drops upon the heads of the mourning crowds. Candles were lit, prayers recited, dried rice placed on foreheads and throats, to give useful insights to be kind to all humans in good deeds and spoken word. The elders prepared a white blanket which they wrapped the boy's body in, when he had arrived at the cremation grounds. Inside were photos and coins which had been placed upon his eyelids for wealth in the next life, along with little mementoes from his short life, such as comic books, words he wrote and pictures he drew. I thought that if I lost my own child, all these precious things would stay with me forever, but then we in the west do not see death as up close and personal as this. The Balinese method of farewell helps the bereaved to say goodbye face-to-face, with the visable realisation that the person really had gone. They believe in cutting all ties; to help the soul move on, as the more you mourn the soul of a loved one, the more the soul will be tied to the earth, unable to return to his original source.

The body had been prepared in the casabo by the town's priests. His mother, sisters, aunties, and grandmothers, several generations of women, carried the body to the front of the home, where the men took over and helped to pull the body up onto the top level of the funeral Badé. This was a tall tower made of wood, specialist paper, gold leaf and craft jewels, with up to nine steps or tiers to heaven, depending on the wealth of the family. Lengths of silk hung down loosely from the top layers, which guide the soul like a pathway out of the body, into Nirvana. Suddenly, the boy's mother broke down, she screamed pure maternal grief for her dead son. Firmly anchoring my lighter spiritual self to the ground, yet at the same time wishing to sprint across the road to console her, I held myself back. An enormous, colourful butterfly fluttered past us all, gently flapping its wings, it hovered around my shoulders.

The butterfly took off in the bereaved mother's direction. Everyone wished to help her to her feet, but the butterfly decided to rest itself upon her outstretched bare leg. Each person present was aware of this one beautiful butterfly and its mystical significance. Total silence prevailed. Just a few individual air molecules bounced around in the sunshine as the sound of delicate wings quivered; these people were very in tune with the spirit. The mother looked up and across the road directly into my struggling eyes, possibly wondering what a white tourist was doing, gate-crashing her son's funeral in the middle of nowhere. She gave a gentle, kind nod and smile, I smiled back. The butterfly remained resting calmly upon her leg, cleaning its delicate wings. Butterflies are symbolic in most religions of new life and rebirth; some believe it is the spirit of the loved one returning to say hello or goodbye for the final time. It flew off up to the tower, still hovering around her son's body, then soared away. It was a special moment. The mother gained new strength as she picked herself up off the floor and carried herself forward to lead the procession, with her saddened husband by her side.

All the village people carried the substantial platform on their bare shoulders; there were no wheels beneath the ton of wood; it was driven on the shoulders of manpower. The men staggered up village roads and pathways, wobbling upon curbs and grass verges. The tower dipped beneath electricity pylons and spun round in dizzy circles at crossroads. This was purposely done, to confuse any malevolent spirits who were trying to steal the young boy's soul before cremation. A small bird was set free from its cage that was hung up high by the side of the Badé to symbolise freedom, everyone cheered. The males of the family carried the Badé three times around the final cremation stand.

The family placed all his earthly belongings beneath the cremation stand, including clothing, schoolbooks, games, bedding, and a pushbike. A gas pipe had been shoved deep into his right flank, which made the coins resting upon his eyes slide off, the gas was turned on and lit. Flames shot around and through his body up to the sky like an ignited oil leak, heat expanding in an invisible cloud. Earth to Earth, ashes to ashes, as the outline of his body became visible through the flames, which crackled, spat, and hissed, then finally dust to dust.

During this incredible fortieth year of travelling the globe, I kept asking myself one, big question throughout, did I wish to change or not to change? Did I need a complete break from tired, repetitive cycles; to abide by newer, clearer, freer ways of being; to rid myself of old restrictive traumas? Did I wish to finally feel the depths of true love? I still, unrealistically, craved to be loved by the people who made me, but knew that was now a fantasy. I knew I needed to breathe deeper, calm my chattering mind more often, relax and enjoy the rest of my precious life and the special people that were on this journey with me. I should probably start to think about settling down, as the batteries inside my biological clock were nearly flat. Believing that there is so much more to this life-of-Claire than living lost, within a herded state; I knew I simply could not function one-moment longer by bleating what everyone else bleats, as I had always been the black ram, wandering lost around the mountains, continually trying to find my way back home.

That fortieth birthday, I realised I had lost my way, and enough was enough. Unavoidable, challenging events became my barometer, a finely-tuned intuition became my torch. This Claire post-birth, once pure in thought and rich in feisty spirit, was a promising and perfect chunk of a newborn baby, who had everything needed within. After my birth was registered, my bond now engrained on paper, this was when all data started to corrupt, becoming lost within the rules and restrictions of childhood. Now I was again ready, re-programmed, fine-tuned, and finally strong enough for re-activation! My out dated perceptions and beliefs had been upgraded, lost creativity and self-confidence reinstated and strengthened. I had not run away from anything during the last two years, thumbing my way around this world; I had simply reclaimed my true Goddess-self. The key was to get out and explore the world and myself at the same time. Of course, I took counsel with many fortune-tellers on my travels and found strangely, most of them mentioned the same thing. "The man of your dreams, someone in uniform, will be coming to claim you as his new wife."

TWELVE

Unity is rare, unique, and sublime
Like a good strong cheese and a glass of wine.

While I was swanning around in my early twenties dressing pop stars, eating out at Michelin star restaurants, clocking up air miles, while travelling the entire planet, I didn't have a single care in this world. Brian, on the other hand had just started a new job as a paramedic, saving the lives of the people of Berkshire. I was forty-two, and Brian was forty-five when our paths crossed. By then, Brian had worked for an ambulance service for twenty-five years, which earned him his first of three medals of service. We met during daylight hours, which for me was unheard of. Since returning from my world trip, I had found employment with a small private ambulance company, but was back on permanent nights (which was killing me already). It was not the most romantic of settings, as our eyes met inside a UTI-scented geriatrics ward within a small specialist hospital.

Brian, the NHS paramedic responder, had called for a backup ambulance to transfer the patient to a bigger hospital with an A&E. My crew mate at the time knew him well, the two of them were having quiet words while I got the patient ready to travel. "What do you think about Brian? He is such a great bloke." My crewmate asked. "Who?" I rudely replied. For me, it was not love at first sight. At this point, my fogged mind did not register that this could be 'the man in uniform,' that everyone from South America to South-East Asia, had recently predicted to be my future husband.

I lived fifty-six miles from my workplace in Bedfordshire, and aside from the long commute, it was a struggle being at work as I really did not wish to do this job anymore. My body spoke to me repeatedly, this time by becoming unwell with rotten adult tonsils. I continued to work through shifts with sweating temperatures, razor blade throat pain, while dealing with abusive drunks and thankfully, more successful maternity calls. I still needed to pay my way, but this was not by any means real living. It seemed impossible to think it was just a few months ago that I trekked for four days to get to Machu Picchu, walked miles along the Great Wall of China, became a Mayan Shaman Priestess in Guatemala, and drank Ayahuasca within the Peruvian jungle with a shaman that whistled like a canary. I was a true free spirit at heart during that time. Now, less than five months after returning to England, here I was again, self-employed, paying bills, stuck on motorways, enslaved inside the repetitive drudgery that is called modern living.

Around two o'clock in the morning, on a warm August night shift, Brian was on station. He shuffled over to the ambulance, as my crewmate and I awaited details of the next emergency call. Brian looked up to the driver's side of the cab. "Hello Claire," was followed by a long awkward pause. "Hello Brian," I replied. Still uncomfortable, he continued. "I wanted to know if you are attached right now, as I would love to take you out sometime?" The garage spotlight shone through the windscreen onto his sweet face. "You want to go out with me?" Even though I had at least two years warning that someone in a green uniform was going to be my husband, his words did not register at all. "I can't, it is complicated, but please don't give up!" It was me who was complicated, had I just turned him down? He spun around and slowly walked away from the ambulance with both clenched hands deep inside his green cargo pockets. I had just shattered his hopes and maybe completely sabotaged both our destinies in one dumb sentence.

The next night shift was my last for a few days. Brian appeared, placing something in my hand. "Thank you, what is it?" I said, slipping it into my trouser side pocket. "I am not giving up, it's for you, as I may not see you again. My time at this station has finished, I am going back to my own station." Brian said this with a deep sense of sorrow in his voice, he lowered his head while his eyes looked up at my face. After battling the rush hour traffic back home where I lived alone, I jumped into my longed-for bed. The thick black pustules had moved in around the back of my throat like mould around a toilet. I had only been back from my grand world tour for five months, and something was going wrong with my life already. During the third afternoon of bedrest, picking up the discarded uniform, checking inside the pockets before I put it in the wash, I found the sealed card that Brian had given me on that last morning. Opening the dusty pink envelope, there was a photograph of a pair of wedged pink flowery flip flops resting on a sun-kissed shoreline somewhere far from England. Inside he said: "Dear Claire, it would be an honour for me to take you out sometime, my phone number is..07...Love Brian XXX." Politely I texted him back, using my latest *Blackberry Storm*, saying thank you and yes, why not, refraining from adding any kisses. His reply was immediate, sounding notably delighted.

The following week, the clouds in the summer sky lied, as it rained and rumbled in streaks of grey and bleak black downpours. How could today be the height of August? Brian had driven over fifty miles and stood on the doorstep drenched, his shoulders upright and square.

Hands outstretched, he handed over the grandest, most exquisite arm full of flowers, while respectfully removing his shoes. He stepped into the living room, quickly he noticed smaller vases of simpler flowers. "Wow," he said as he looked around the room. "You know, my mother Sally once told me that if I ever enter a home full of flowers, I would know that this is where love lives." The irony was, I did indeed love flowers and all things creative and beautiful, I just did not love myself.

On the 1st of March, earlier that same year of 2010, after a long and painful six-year battle with stomach cancer, Brian's mother Sally had passed away aged sixty-seven. He spoke emotively and honestly about her life. I could see he was deep in grief with her recent passing. He explained that his dad had died suddenly a few years earlier, also aged sixty-seven. Brian had recently been living alone in a single nurses' residence due to his previous marriage breakdown. He shared that they had a seventeen-year-old son. Six weeks into our new romance, since things were going well, I asked him to pack his bags and move in with me. He moved one carrier bag of mismatched clothing, along with a million boxes of heavy metal vinyl records, CD's, rockumentary DVDs, and a half-opened box with a green plastic urn with Sally's ashes in it. It seemed that his mother was moving in with us.

One night we were watching a film, suddenly there was an almighty crash. A framed photograph of Kylie had somehow fallen off the inner wall from the kitchen, then had flown backwards landing on the floor in front of us, completely intact. "There she is Brian!" I exclaimed, "that's your Mum saying hello, she is here!" Brian looked at me as if I was insane. The perfect landing of the picture frame was a logistical impossibility. Brian became pale but was in deep thought. "How about we scatter her ashes soon, maybe she wants to break free?" I suggested.

Looking up at the lonely green urn on the shelf above, he agreed. A few days later, Brian had prepared himself to let his mother go. He suggested that she be scattered by a Lebanese cedar, which he and his family had planted in her honour a few months before. The tree was in Dorney Lake by Eton, where they had lived as a family for many years. Derek, a dear friend of his father's, and a forester by trade lived nearby. He would regularly attend to the tree, making sure it was kept in perfect condition.

Brian and I stood by the tree, we said a prayer and let her ashes go. It was a deeply emotional time for him. As we mindfully walked away, Brian handed the green urn to me. "Do you think you could get rid of this? I don't know what to do with it anymore, I cannot bear to throw her in the bin." It felt as if the urn was in some way still part of Sally. "Of course, I can, don't you worry." Unscrewing the urn slowly, I looked inside. There were some remaining ashes collected at the bottom, along with a card, with her full name, birth, and death dates, with her cremation details, all beautifully handwritten in calligraphy ink. When we got home, I put the urn under the bed and forgot about it. Derek, the forester, returned to the Cedar tree, shortly after we had left, to clear it of Sally's ashes, as this would have poisoned the tree.

Six weeks after Brian had moved in, panic struck. This had nothing to do with having to listen to heavy metal music day and night, but more to do with his soft nature, and his overwhelming kindness. This was so contradictory to anything I was used to; my response was irrational. One Saturday afternoon, I suffered a wobble and walked out of the house, telling him to move somewhere else as I could not cope any more. I left him half-baked in a state of sheer confusion. Driving over to see my friend Lucy, who lived nearby, my heart and mouth did not coordinate very well. "But Lucy, he is too perfect; I can't stand it any longer." I uttered while trying to imagine collecting my

Golden Globe award. "What do you mean, too perfect, Claire? Have you gone mad? Where is he now, what's he done that is too right?" Lucy looked as if she was seconds away from laughing. Apparently, this was not a normal thing, to say that someone was too perfect. "He is at home, cooking us both lunch from scratch." Now I was finding it hard to keep a straight face myself. "You see, he buys fresh cut flowers every week, without fail, and expensive ones with water pouches attached. What bugs me is he keeps saying that he loves me, even on our first date, what does this all mean?"

"It means he loves you. Have you said you love him back at all? It's been a good few months now." She asked, tilting one eyebrow. "No, and it's only been twelve weeks," I rebutted. Thinking to myself, how could I not love this man, he was in one word, perfect. "Now listen to me, you go back home, then sit down at the table and enjoy what he has cooked for you while enjoying his company, his love, and the flowers with pouches, and his kindness because you deserve all of this. I have never seen you happier, and Brian is a lovely, kind, and hilarious man. He makes me laugh, and that is a good thing." With that, Lucy pushed me out the door. While in the car driving home, I mulled it all over, as I remembered I was not fifteen anymore. Walking through the front door, something smelt divine, thankfully he had not left. Sheepishly I said how sorry I was, and how glad I was that he had not given up on me.

A few months later, we decided to move to Berkshire. This made sense, as commuting over a hundred miles a day in two different cars, just because we worked opposite shifts, was becoming impossible and expensive. As I was clearing out the house, I came across Sally's urn. Not wanting to upset Brian, I pondered what I should do with it. By now, I also did not want to just throw her in the bin, as she was becoming very much part of our relationship, but I could not leave it at just any old place. It was the funeral director's card that got me in a heart-wrench tizzy. The first anniversary of Sally's death was coming up in March 2011. Brian asked sometime in February, what I had done with the urn? "Oh yes, I forgot to say before, I recently found a beautiful woodland nearby, full of snowdrops, I buried her there." I told my first lie. "Gosh, that is so you." Brian said. So, I had to move fast on this before he found it.

The next day I went to work on the ambulance doing a patient transfer. Sally was coming with us. My crewmate for the day was Mark, he had known about all my spooky escapades for many years, so this story was nothing new to him. In fact, he found it all quite funny. We took turns driving all the way up from Slough, Berkshire to Morpeth, Northumberland, both of us looking out for anywhere to leave Sally. In the end, we found nowhere appropriate in plain view, as the ambulance was tracked. We had picked our patient up from a care home. She was ninety-seven and clearly coming to the end of her life. She had dementia along with other more severe health conditions, her body was failing her. There was no doubt that she was on her final journey to a Hospice in Barnstable, North Devon. I made her comfortable, then sat opposite her, so I could keep an eye on her throughout the trip.

A few hours into the journey, the lights in the ambulance started flickering. I ignored it at first, but then the bulbs began flashing on and off. I shouted through to Mark. "Are you messing with the lights?" Mark called back. "I'm not doing anything. Maybe it's the ghost of Sally!" I could see his eyes, wide and mocking in the rear-view mirror as he continued along the motorway. The lights in the back went off, then they came back on again. I joked, "It looks like Sally's not too keen on your driving." The old lady had just woken up. "Who's Sally?" She asked. "Is that her there?" Pointing to the empty seat behind me.

"Is she coming with us? She says she is from Liverpool. I loved *The Beatles*!" I was not expecting that reply, I knew it was Sally, who was indeed from Liverpool. It was not surprising the old lady could see her. Often, at the end of life, we see through to the other side. The lights flickered again. Now I knew for sure that the spirit of Brian's mum was with us, on this, our patient's and now Sally's final journey. "Yes," I said, smiling. "She's called Sally, and she's coming with us." Knowing Brian's mother was travelling along with us inspired me to jot down a note to her, so I grabbed a patient report form and poured out my heart to her on the back of it.

It took six hours to get to the hospice. Once we had dropped the patient off into her room, we were offered tea and cake. I noticed the head of a rose on the floor next to the table that I was sitting at and bent down to pick it up, thinking that I could put it in Sally's urn. A nurse saw me and smiled quizzically, so I felt compelled to tell her what I was doing. She suggested, "Why don't you hold a ceremony in the courtyard of the hospice?" She went to get the managers approval, returning with an armful of roses from the garden. I got the urn from the ambulance, then broke up all the roses into petals and popped them inside the urn. Back in the hospice courtyard, opening the urn, removing the card, I put it with the note I had written to Sally in my pocket. We all said a prayer as I scattered the remaining ashes, along with the rose petals, onto a flowerbed. The manager offered to dispose of the empty urn, so I handed all responsibility to her. On the 1st of March 2011, the first anniversary of Sally's death, I told Brian the whole story. I thought he would be annoyed with me, but he gave me a big hug and told me how grateful he was that I had given his mum such a beautiful, second send-off.

Not long after we moved to Berkshire, I became plagued with overwhelming maternal feelings. My every thought was of starting a family. This was a new, even scarier place to be than being in love. Why was I becoming obsessed about motherhood at this grand old age of forty-three? Meeting Brian, I knew I had found the father to my children, as he was the most incredibly devoted father to his now eighteen-year-old son. He fully supported his son's development into adulthood. Oddly, at times this made me feel so sad, realising how much my own father had neglected my every need. Witnessing such unconditional love from Brian to his son, I knew I had to follow every byway, search high and low, check out every path I knew, ford every stream, climb every mountain, and follow the rainbow's end in search of my future happiness.

Before we created a child, there was a deep desire to work diligently through all my maternal psychological blocks, one by one. I had forgotten to wind up my biological clock in my mid-thirties, which was clearly stuck on yesterday's timeline. Forty years' worth of buried, confusing issues needed to surface, be explored, accepted then let go. I went on fad diets, walked more, recited offertory chants in almost monophonic undertones as I sang out my exasperation to do with family life, breathing in the acceptance and love felt from the man who I was now on this journey with. He ate his way through bottles of zinc, devoured more green leafy vegetables with his meat pies, and reluctantly cut down on real ale.

After eight months, nothing was happening. Our doctor investigated further. All blood tests came back borderline geriatric. First, my Follicle-Stimulating Hormone (which is produced by the pituitary gland in the brain), was deficient. This is the primary hormone for reproduction, it is a supporter of growth in ovarian follicles and in the maturation of the eggs during ovulation, by stimulating the ovarian follicles. Secondly, to make things worse and for me to feel even less of a childbearing woman, the Anti-Mullerian Hormone levels, would confirm if I had any viable ovarian eggs on reserve. This smart little hormone prevents the maturation of eggs all at the same time, a kind of turnstile of the reproductive system. They too were the lowest recorded level. The third, and final, humiliation was the Antral Follicle Count which again reiterated that I had very few eggs left in my coop. All the female eggs have been formed within our ovaries by the time we are born, these eggs strengthen and evolve as we hit puberty, then start to decay with age. The antral follicle is a resting follicle which looks like a tiny sac filled with fluid, this part accommodates an immature egg. These eggs were very mature since we had all recently shared our forty-third year together.

As if this day could not get any worse, my old body was oestrogen dominant, meaning my progesterone levels were dangerously low. The nurse asked if my periods were irregular, which they were every 35 to 45 days! She told me that the body needs a higher progesterone level for the first twelve weeks of foetal life, as this feeds the baby while the placenta is being created. That is why many women miscarry during those first twelve weeks. The fertility nurse suggested that I should not get my hopes up, at forty-three, I was already too old.

This was the grand finale, for which I took my final bow. Even though Brian was the perfect partner, it was too late to start a family. Despondently I surrendered the brief but fanciful dream of ever being a mother. Due to my abysmal test results proving my ovarian reserve had dried up, IVF might still be my only chance of pregnancy. I would need an array of daily Marian devotions to make that happen, but even after any kind of divine intervention, helped along with twenty-first-century science, could I keep the pregnancy safe to full term?

That left adoption or fostering as our only option at this stage. The nurse had written a charming follow-up report to my GP saying those same blunt cutting words. Brian, on the other hand, aged forty-six, had one sperm test which came back a 100% healthy. "We can do this together, we will go private, let us keep trying. Anyway, what did you say to me when I asked you out, and you turned me down? Don't give up!"

"But darling, my entire reproductive arena is now completely bandless, how will going private bring the crowds back to the festival? It is too late; you cannot make this happen. I must come to terms with the fact I am not worthy of a family of my own in any capacity." My mood darkened, sinking ever deeper into the crazy murky depths of spinsterhood. What had I been doing all these years? My family messed up my beginnings, which set the scene for my insecurities of relationships and babies. I was irresponsible in keeping a foetus alive in my twenties, and committed to nobody during my thirties, since the thoughts of being a housewife, plagued me with dread.

I had always had a mental blackout about pregnancy. My mother used to gossip to strangers that she knew I would be pregnant by the time I was thirteen, but thirteen passed by with no baby. At fourteen, fifteen, then sixteen, then throughout my absence at home, Rita screamed louder than ever via extremely tenuous jungle drums, almost placing certain bets that I would end up on the streets, taking drugs and pregnant. Well, sixteen also passed, and yes, I could have ended up on the streets if it were not for my team of helpers, natural artistic drive and determination and communicative talents which, undoubtedly, saved me. There was no drug addiction and no babies. Subconsciously, I had embedded deep into my teen psyche, that I would never allow myself to become pregnant, just so Rita could not say 'I told you so!' This was serious, I needed to seek hypnotherapy to unlock the baby block.

I felt useless as a female, suddenly realising that I had focused too much on my working life and enjoying my freedom. Brian continued to work non-stop and carried on drinking his real ales on the sly. We decided to move. We found a perfect secluded cottage, but it had no mobile phone signal, as neither of us thought to check that on viewing. Internet became non-existent as my *Samsung Galaxy S* could not pick up one single bar of the world wide web.

Winter drew in, around November we both worked an ambulance shift together around West London, where we were dealing with a very frail, elderly lady who had lost her mind completely. She was a risk to herself, needing to be admitted into the hospital. Brian had jumped ahead and got into the back of the ambulance to get things ready. I climbed up into the ambulance, missing the step entirely, thanks to my bootlace being undone. My body fell sideways onto the road below, it flew into the air like a goalkeeper missing the ball at a cup final. My shoulder smashed on the ground first, followed by my head that hit the tarmac below with a thud. My right ankle twisted quite badly. The old lady was, thankfully, stationary on the ground and bound up safe in the carry chair. "CLAIRE, are you alright?" Brian yelled as he lunged forward to help. "Help me up, let's get her in and settled before anyone with a smart phone sees this and we end up on flipping YouTube." I managed to say coherently while feeling semi-concussed. I was seen by A&E as a priority, an x-ray was taken, which showed extensive tearing of ligaments in my right ankle. Our working day was over, and my life would never be the same again.

THIRTEEN

The fragments of life soar
Bathed in the firmament of wonder.

Over the years, I had learnt how to adapt and cope with the reality that my birth family would never be a support system for me. Imagine finding yourself tied into a non-negotiable lifetime contract of bloodlines, who all appear, in principle, to be the best family I could endure for deep soul learning. An entire family, including spiteful siblings, came to assist me in being a stronger, more independent, resourceful, quick thinking, and interesting survivor of life. Their only tasks were to be oblivious to the basic needs of a small child, highly critical during early development stages, irresponsible even neglectful in action throughout school life, then spitefully absent during all accomplishments that followed thereafter. Still, I never gave up hoping there was someone nearby who cared. Apart from Michael, my dear neighbour from the Kings Cross era of 1991, who was by now more of a dad to me than Arthur ever was, there was Brenda. She was Rita's (part-time) best friend, who was becoming more of a mother to me as time went by. Brenda and Rita's friendship went back to when they were both teenagers working in Peter Jones shoe department in the King's Road, Chelsea. The one thing Brenda would say to everyone about me was, "I used to feed her a bottle and read her stories." This single-minded woman had been with me since birth; no one else alive could ever claim this devotion.

During 1987, when I was twenty years old and moved back down to London from the North-East, I connected further with Brenda as she was now only a tube journey away. Brenda believed in angels, the afterlife, as she was a fellow Aquarian, who loved that we shared this planetary connection. Whenever I was in any kind of difficulty, Brenda's first words would be, "It's because you are an Aquarian and we don't behave in ways others would like us to." Either by design or by chance, she became my surrogate. When I was experiencing life's difficulties, Brenda was there to balance things out, sharing all my heartbreaks and celebrations.

Brenda supported most of my crazy ideas, hairstyles, partners, and career choices. We usually had heated yet healthy debates. She did her damnedest to help patch things up with my family, especially with her friend Rita; but she often tore out her perfectly coiffed, white, permed hair at Rita's continued small-mindedness. When Brenda turned eighty, she became sick with breast cancer, I was devastated. She was the first person I was close to who had cancer; she was not someone I had picked up in the ambulance. This was too real for me. Brenda was never a bedridden-type of a sick person, even though she often complained of aches and pains. After a year battling with chemo, it spread into secondary lung cancer. Throughout, she was incredibly independent, insisting she make her own way to her many oncology appointments, using her free bus pass. Her oncology team had arranged for much-needed rest periods at Hospice.

One Saturday afternoon, when Brian and I were working on the ambulance; my intuitive gut said all was not well. The tumours were spreading; she had been taken into Hospice that morning by ambulance. When

I phoned her, she sounded dreadful, there was a distinct crackling breathlessness to her voice as she gasped for air. Brenda adored Michael, my King's Cross comrade, but now she also loved Brian. She struggled to say that she wished to share a moment with him on the phone. "Brian love, please, will you look after my Claire, she is a lovely girl, and I adore her like she is my own, promise me now?" He said he would to the end of time, it was as if she was handing over the baton. For the following ten days, we kept vigil at the Hospice. Dabbing her cracked lips with a lollipop sponge soaked in mineral water, I avidly recited all the weird and wonderful stories of my journey in life since I was a kid, which is the time when she fondly remembered me the most.

There were seven vibrant scented Gerberas, one for each day of the week, displayed sparingly in a solid glass vase with fresh water on her bedside table. "I have said this to you before Claire, but I will repeat this." Her breathing became laboured. "I am proud to have known you all your life." A long pause hung dormant in the air. "I cannot believe you are forty-three. I remember when you were born, damn your bloody mother has missed out here, but I am so glad I have not." She said trying to inhale air into her failing lungs. "Wow, Brenda, thank you for being my everything." I meant every word; she was my everything. "Well my dear, it needs to be said, you have been through enough. Your family are complete flipping idiots." It was hard for her to breathe and talk at the same time, but I understood every word, especially the 'flipping idiots' bit.

When I was small and vulnerable, Brenda did indeed feed me my bottle and read stories. Now it was my turn, giving her a baby tumbler and reciting our life stories. I looked down at her on the bed, realising how tiny and frail she had become with cancer and age. I felt the same sense of pride toward her as she spoke about me. The ever-evolving cycle of life and death presented itself to me that day. "I will have words when I get to Heaven, especially when your parents get there. I will be waiting for them, mark my words!" I knew she would, especially my dad. I think she had a lifelong crush on him too. "Brian is a good man; you must allow him to love you. You must open that protected heart of yours and feel happy. I know it is not long till I leave this world, I am not scared you know. We have both always understood what is coming next, I will just be returning home. You have been a great daughter to me, at least your mother gave me this." This was the last lucid conversation we ever had; she was starting to let go. Her powerful words atoned for many years of abandonment from my family. "Brenda, say hello to everyone Heaven side for me." I knew she would. "You bet I will. Also, I am going to have words about getting you and Brian a baby; it is never too late. My sister had Izzy at 43, they coped perfectly fine and look how amazing my niece is now." I did not expect that. Izzy, her niece, was with us throughout this time of her passing.

One warm, clear evening, as the sun contemplated the colours to dress the evening in, we observed the fresh flowers in the room as they absorbed their last drops of moisture. The soft limp petals, struggling to stay alive, began to orchestrate their final descent. The synchronicity of how nature mirrored human life, was acknowledged by all of us in the room. A fox tapped his nose upon the glass patio windows, he looked in for a second then left. Stooping down, I kissed her warm baby soft skin, and said goodbye.

By the end of that day, the petals from the Gerbera's began to break away, their stiff stems weakened from the top-down, hunching slowly to the narrow table below. The water in the vase had been absorbed and the vase started to smell off. The dried petals fell further to the ground below; like freshly burst balloons. The morphine was increased. Brenda said her goodbyes in her own way, her hand did not respond to my squeezes anymore.

Momentarily my forehead rested wearily on the hospital bed; when I felt the new kind of energy coming from Brenda's limp hand. Taking a moment: wondering where her spirit was right then; was she preparing herself, was she in there sleeping, could she not move her body, but could hear me like I heard the ambulance men many years before? What was she feeling, if anything at all? Suddenly, she raised herself up from her stack of pillows, both her arms reaching out rigidly in front, both eyes opened fully for the first time in days. "Are you all right? What's going on?" I asked as I stood up beside her, wondering if I should press the alarm. A voice, which was not hers of late, came booming out of her mouth. "Yes, I am coming; I am coming, wait, wait for me. I am ready, take me home." With that, Brenda closed her eyes and laid herself back into her upright position. Her breathing returned to being intensely laboured as her lungs slowly filled with fluids. Brian, Izzy, and her boyfriend Shaun returned from the tearoom. They said I looked as if I had seen a ghost, maybe I just had?

A few days later, Izzy and I spent an evening at the funeral home, decorating Brenda's Eco-cardboard coffin. This was a new, cheaper option in the world of funerals. The idea of decorating the cardboard box came from the Bali boy's, whose cremation I attended while travelling. We stuck everything Brenda on to the outside of the box, such as postcards of her beloved Cornwall, and pictures of owls that we had had no idea she loved so much. We both rewrote poems and verses sent in by loved ones, in coloured felt pen. Her friends had sent all-things-Brenda they wanted to add inside her coffin. There was nothing received from my parents at all. Still, we stuck all of it outside the box. It was cathartic, almost a childlike meditation, to be sitting in a quiet funeral home, as we coloured in, cut out, and pasted on while mindfully reminiscing about her life.

Brenda had graciously allowed me to walk her through her death experience, from her first diagnosis to her beautiful passing, and now onward to her cremation. This was such an enormous experience which no classroom could ever have taught. We should spend more time with our dying and dead, to say goodbye. As an adult, I had not only learnt how to save a life, I had now learnt how to honour death.

FOURTEEN

I will restart anew and refresh my soul.
Castaway the clouds and again be whole.

Our remote hilltop Hamlet must have been the quietest place on the planet; you could hear thoughts quite clearly with no fewer than nine decibels all around us. I was stranded and partially immobilised for six weeks, due to a foolish ankle injury, thanks to falling out of an ambulance. This lifestyle was not going to pay the rent. Wearing an air-walker physio boot, walking became a challenge, I was fast becoming very reliant on Brian for the duration of my recovery. I was frustrated with everything; limited phone signal, no local shop, no petrol station for emergency supplies, and no internet for home deliveries (and no Netflix, as it had not been invented yet.)

Frequently it snowed, which added to my isolation. Brian could not get into work over a few sub-arctic days due to the heavy snowfall. Our bendy, one-track road had not been gritted, as it was too narrow for a lorry to climb. We were snowed in. So, making the best of our time off together, we binge-watched box sets on DVD. One sub-zero evening, Brian had gone back to work a twelve-hour night shift on the ambulance. My eyes became heavy, I turned off the bedside lamp, then saw odd beams of light bouncing around the ceiling and walls; the bedroom was usually pitch black. The moon was waxing, snow-covered lawns bounced light back up to the sky, but there was nothing outside to explain these lights. Lying entirely still, with my injured leg resting upon a few stacked pillows, both eyes wide open, I caught sight of perfect light orbs. Each one swathed with vibrant colours (some I could not describe), they danced through the darkness, perfectly married like a spotlight to a disco ball. After twenty minutes, it all stopped, the room returned to total darkness.

The following morning, when Brian had returned from his night shift, we swapped bed places. I went into the bathroom, where a loud voice in my head urged me to do a pregnancy test. Bursting into muffled laughter, reminding myself what the hard-faced fertility nurse had said, just a couple of years back, that at forty-three I was too old to conceive. Now suddenly forty-five, and a bit more on the stocky side through lack of exercise, thanks to my ankle infliction, this was an impossibility. Brian was now forty-eight, so even in my optimistic mind, we were absolutely past it. Nonetheless, I succumbed, since there had always been that one per cent of me that got me through this life so far, I remained still hopeful. Reaching into my bathroom drawer, pulling out an in-date digital test stick, I did the test. I waited.

It beamed positive! Apparently, I was already a mummy by three weeks, and a big smiley face proved it. Was this right? I rechecked the expiry date, it was all OK. Brian was awake. I hobbled into the bedroom, my right lower leg wearing a single sock of yellow and green sorrow. The swelling was significantly reduced; and the boot was off, as I was on the ascent back to normality. I stood in front of him, beaming. "You will never guess what?" Unable to contain my joy a second longer, I pulled out the stick from behind my back and showed him the digital screen. Neither of us could believe it. We were going to have a baby at our grand old ages. My lazy follicles had woken up, and in doing so, had poached to perfection those non-viable eggs.

That same glorious December morning, already three weeks into being a mother, just after Brian had gone back to bed, the postman handed me a parcel that I recognised. After Brenda had died, Brian and I hosted a charity event to raise money for Trinity Hospice, where Brenda had passed away. Brian had already created an event called Mearfest in the name of his mother, Sally Mear. Together, we raised over two thousand pounds in one night, and the event was a success. I created a photo book in Brenda's memory, with everything Brenda and Mearfest within, naïvely thinking it would be an ice-breaker to send to my mother, after twenty-odd years of silence. It was a fitting tribute to her lifetime friend, who she never saw, especially while she was dying of cancer during the last two years of her life. Rita, in her ruthlessness, had posted it right back to me, 'Return to Sender'. My heart sank, on the most incredible day of my life, when I was to finally join the rather sought-after club of mums, the very woman who carried me for forty-one weeks and five days, had tried to destroy this day too. My hormones were at a loss as to what to do next. They had never worked so hard as they were doing that day. I cried, holding my belly with both hands cradled together, promising our baby, that I would never abandon it, not until the day I died. Even then I would guide it from beyond the ozone, which Brenda had clearly done for us, as she had kept her absolute promise of a baby.

The doctor confirmed a positive result with an HCG blood test, proving I was a middle-aged primigravida. At the twelve-week nuchal translucency scan, we could see our little creature of joy moving around inside. The scan showed nothing wrong with the baby, its neck and nose measured perfect, so far there were no structural abnormalities. We were advised to have the amniocentesis test, to check if the baby had Down, Edwards or Patau syndrome. This was a standard test, as there is a higher chance of chromosomal issues the older the eggs are, and let us face it, my eggs were no spring chickens. The midwife consultant took us aside. She advised that there was a new test, which was not as invasive as the amniocentesis. This relatively new test (2013) was called a Harmony blood test, which was available privately, and she suggested we investigate further.

Two days after my forty-sixth birthday, we moved house again, during a Valentine's Day blizzard. The new house had an impressive, glass-vaulted sunroof, on which the snow settled in thick layers. Underneath lay an open-plan living, dining, and kitchen space with wood flooring, enough space for a baby to learn to crawl safely while I kept a beady eye on it. We were situated in a more friendly Oxfordshire village, potentially with mother-and-baby groups, and everything practical that an older parent would need with a young baby. I was already a moderate size, savouring every minute of being pregnant. This was a baby who had miraculously made its way to this stage of life, with nearly zero help from my lazy ovarian hormone team. It had defied all medical odds. I loved it the minute that stick smiled. My life and our baby's life had been planned out for the next thirty years at least, assuming we made it to seventy-five years of age.

Our baby had just turned eighteen weeks when we arrived at a reputable fertility clinic in central London. The doctor took my blood for the Harmony test, and we received an in-depth scan as part of the procedure. He asked if we wanted to know the sex? Both of us had been praying for a girl. Brian had a grown-up son, so he wished for a daughter this time. The doctor's face lit up; she was a girl! The doctor looked at the scan, checking her measurements, informing us that all looked normal and well. We could see her moving, instantly falling in love with her. The doctor explained that the blood test would determine 99% accurately if she has Down syndrome.

One springtime morning, I wandered through the high street, when the name Molly flooded my mind. Spotting a book in a shop window with Molly in the title. I then noticed in the next street a cleaning van with Molly as its name, written clearly on the side panel. Was someone talking to me? "Brian, what do you think of the name Molly? As I sent my text, I received his text at the same time. "I just thought of the name Molly or Emily, what do you think? :0 XXXX" Sent from his rather primitive flip lid *Nokia 6101*. From day one he always finished with a million kisses. Molly it was.

Two weeks had passed since the blood test; baby Molly had just turned twenty weeks. I was so happy, truly happy for the first time in my life, I felt true love for Brian who never gave up on us. I felt the most vibrant I had ever been, with the smoothest clearest skin that glowed with health and contentment. It was all thanks to this amazing life, growing to her perfect centile. Brian, on the other hand, had developed severe back pain during the night before, he became crippled by it, having to take a rare day off work. The digital cordless home phone rang. It was the clinic, asking if I was sitting down, which did not sound right.

"Can I call you, Claire?" She asked in a controlled, calm voice. "Of course." I said, as bile slowly made its way up to my semi-choked throat, which is now my trusted bad news barometer. "Claire, I have good news and bad news for you today." That did not sound good; leaning more towards the bad news my heart already started to sink. "The good news is your baby does not have Trisomy 18, otherwise known as Edwards syndrome. This is when babies can die just before or just after birth, it is not life-sustaining." She paused; I thought that was great news. I felt relieved. "The other good news is your baby is low risk for Trisomy 13 or Patau syndrome. This is another chromosomal condition, associated with severe intellectual disability and physical abnormalities in many parts of the body, only 1% of babies born with this live to one year old." So far, this was two bits of good news, all excellent, then she said. "OK, so the bad news is your baby is 99% positive for Trisomy 21, which is Down syndrome. Your baby has an extra chromosome." She paused again. I clutched at my chest in panic, trying to figure out how percentages worked in my head. "Claire, are you still there?"

"Yes, so there is still a full 1% chance she doesn't have Down syndrome?" The blood drained from my cheeks pooling down around my ankles, held in by chunky Matalan flip flops. Brian started shaking as his back pain increased. It was clear there was a problem, Brian had somehow sensed this earlier on.

"I'm sorry, Claire, but 99% is pretty much concrete that your baby has this condition." Her tone stayed the same throughout, not too high pitched nor monotonous, a steady medium. "We need to talk about how to proceed with this pregnancy. You must discuss this with Mr Mear and your consultants, then let us know what you wish to do. It is not too late to terminate the pregnancy, or we can offer genetic counselling and additional testing if you both see fit."

"How could I possibly abort our baby now? Not now, she is a baby, our miracle, who had no Down syndrome markers on the many previous scans so far, including her twenty-week anomaly, this has to be a big mistake?" My voice was breaking, along with my heart. How did this happen? A silent pause came from both ends of the phone line. "These tests are 99% accurate Claire; they are never wrong." She confirmed as I screamed something that sounded like the beginnings of fighting talk down the phone. Brian looked visibly shaken at my response, as I dropped the phone on the floor, kicking it away with my weakened right leg, which was the primary reason we were in this mess. Brian struggled to pick the phone up from the floor, he politely spoke to the Grim Reaper, then hung up.

We called our consultant, who was profoundly shocked and as equally baffled at the results. She booked us in for the very next day. She measured Molly over and over, taking her time, getting second opinions. She felt this was not the right diagnosis, but our doubts would not go away from that moment forward. And so, with heavy hearts, we accepted the possible outcome that she would need assistance throughout her life. Perhaps we were the right parents to cope with her physical condition. Maybe, as we were older and medically trained and spiritually tuned in, we were chosen for her journey? I felt happy to change direction and be a full time, stay-at-home mother to Molly for the rest of my life. We would have to wait for another twenty weeks, until full-term, to find out the full extent of this. What had those double-crossing baby Hellions within this messed up Multiverse been playing at?

This information attracted new people into our lives, new mystic friends and so-called healers joined our journey into parenthood, now with the possibility of a special need's baby. I was Dorothy being swept along a mystical *Jaune de Brique*, I felt more like my crazy mother than ever before. Some spoke to the angels on my behalf; they became a conduit between my new special need's child and the Heavens. The gurus explained that we were fully protected, as they chanted to their guides and Gods, stating Molly would be born as a special spirit of high frequency. A healthy baby girl with just twenty normal chromosomes, all will be fine, but who wanted normal?

The weeks dragged by. Molly had grown to the perfect centile; our baby daughter was doing well. No one showed any other concerns; the regular midwife dipped my urine and found my glucose and protein levels were normal. Everyone at the hospital continued to focus on the Harmony blood test with its ridiculous, false-positive results, for they could not see past it. Mid-June, at thirty-two weeks, we drove fifty miles to attend an outside Country Fayre. Sitting amongst all kinds of petting-farm animals, and pony gymkhanas with school-age kids competing, there sat a solitary tarot reader; his name was Peter. Like a cooing homing pigeon, I flapped around the perimeter of his standard British caravan, with its infinity awning erected at the front. Then, like a psychic zombie, I handed over five pounds.

Shuffling the cards, I could ask one question. "Is my baby going to be OK, will she be born healthy?" Hoping I would get away with two questions in one. "When are you due?" Peter asked, placing the cards face down on the table. "Eight weeks." He started to glance underneath each card, then flipped them all face-up. "Ummm, can you shuffle again." Peter handed back the cards, I knew a second shuffle could not be good news. "Well, it's a girl, but there is a problem. She has a condition that you have battled with greatly in your own heart. This is not a favourable outcome." He stopped talking and sighed. "Meaning?" I prodded for another £3.50 worth of answer. "Well, meaning, I see you returning to the hospital a few times in the coming weeks. Your baby is very poorly, she will need medical intervention and a lot of faith on your part. I am sorry not to bring you better news, but I say what I see. Do you have any other questions?" I guessed that this was about four pounds and twenty pence worth of an answer. I continued, "She has Down syndrome, which we are coming to terms with, but it is questionable if she does have it at all." I tried to get my full fivers worth. "This is not up to me; it is in the lap of the Gods. She is a unique baby, a special girl, not particularly special needs. No, I am just being told 'special,' I see that she will help many people in her lifetime." His final words implied that she would make it, she was special already, a miracle. I guess she did have Down syndrome. "God bless you and your baby girl."

We attended fortnightly scans, to check, double-check and triple-check her safe arrival. Monday 5th August 2013, Molly was thirty-nine weeks exactly when the head cardiologist consultant had taken forty-five minutes to super-check her heart. The most common cardiac anomaly for T21 is a ventricular septal defect. Congenital heart disease (CHD) is frequently described in patients with Down syndrome and is the leading cause of death during the first two years of life. The Down syndrome spectrum of CHD patterns varies worldwide; this deviation could be due to geographic, genetic, and sociodemographic aspects. Two senior cardiac experts confirmed Molly's heart to be robust; with a steady, strong pulse with no visible heart disease or ventricular defects. Her measurements were perfect; she was already in the right position for her descent. There was enough amniotic fluid, and her placenta looked in a favourable position with plenty of blood flow.

How can she be poorly? I chose to let go of Peter the tarot readers predictions. Everything was greenlit; we were ready to go. We had gone from zero confidence in ever being able to conceive, to carrying Molly for two hundred and eighty days of uncertainty, stress, and worry. The consultant reiterated that she did not wish for us to go beyond the fortieth-week, not even by one day. Monday 12th August 2013 was that day, making it very clear there would be no birthing pool, as I am at high risk and Molly may need medical attention (but she doubted this.)

Urine had been dipped by my midwife on Wednesday 7th August, there were no signs of glucose, diabetes, proteins, pre-eclampsia, and no kidney infections. I had a stretch and sweep that made me feel queasy, however, I was good to go. Molly's heartbeat sounded alive on the expensive midwifes' foetal doppler, like an harras of Stallions galloping through the Glen. Molly was engaged in the downward anterior position. Thursday morning, an unfamiliar queasiness engulfed my auric field. I wondered if she was moving enough, thinking this was probably normal at thirty-nine weeks and four days. Drinking fluids was my priority, resting an impossibility, believing that in three days' time it would all be over.

FIFTEEN

We chose not to remember her with flowers
Or marking time in minutes and hours.

It certainly was all over. Molly did not make it. Within a week of giving birth to a lifetime of bereavement, I could not sit at home all day long. My friends found it hard to pop by and say hello. Hours after Molly died, Brian went back to work on the ambulances, it was his only coping mechanism. After a week (that seemed like a year), I also returned to work on the ambulances. Our first shift together fell on a Sunday.

The primary job of the day was to assist a lady living around the corner from Royal Berkshire hospital, who had a PV (per vagina) bleed and was clearly miscarrying. Ambulance Control had no idea who we were, or that I had given birth to a full-term stillborn just days before in this area. It was a marvel I could even fit into the green ambulance uniform, let alone drive on blue lights and continue to smile, then deal with strangers' worst days, while suffering ghastly haemorrhoids that were the size of Ayers Rock. These emergency callers thought they were having a bad day, if only they knew! Calling upon my semi-redundant seventy-six shamanic Mayan angel guides and To Keep Watch, who I spoke with often these days, I asked them to show up and give us both a hand to get us through the day shift ahead. At the address, a distraught husband answered the door, speaking in broken English. Brian asked how we could help; you cannot make this up!

"My wife, she twenty-four weeks pregnant, IVF baby, our last hope, bleeding and in pain," he said as he hurried us both to the upstairs bedroom. Skimming through her maternity notes, subtly I began to take over from Brian, talking her through her options, checking her vitals before we got her into the ambulance. Once at the hospital, it was protocol that she went straight to the labour ward, as she was over twenty-one weeks. The midwives behind the desk did a double-take. They asked why we were there and in uniform? Good question, I had no clue why we were there, just days after our own loss, but my heart was one hundred per cent with our patient that day. I knew double her pain, along with all the other mothers I had assisted in my career as a medic. We were all members of the same rotten club of stillbirth.

During the height of the 2013 British summer; the heat had reached unimaginable temperatures. Molly was nine days old and still being dissected, weighed, and tissue-sampled onto slides. Their findings were written up into official and unofficial classified reports, this data added to regional, national, and international statistics on the causes and preventions of stillbirth in women in their mid-forties. We decided we had to get out of the house and get some air, so we visited another country show. Like an extra from a Michael Jackson Thriller video I limped my way over to a regular gypsy caravan, heading straight for it. I admit to being a born and bred gypsy junky. The sandwich board outside the caravan door said her name was Gypsy Leigh, nice twist to an old favourite. Her tariff was £5 a question, £10 for a standard reading, £40 for a full reading including a light show from the crystal ball itself, with a good luck charm thrown in.

"Good Morning to you, my dear one." Gypsy Leigh was an older woman with a complexion that dated back to the early seventies. The distinct lifelines on her face told me her story, through a cover of bronze pan-stick foundation, waves of Neptune blue eye tones had been skilfully applied with a cheese knife. Thin lips had been drenched in Boris Karloff gloss, which bled seamlessly into her upper smoker lines. Her natural white hair had streaks of nicotine sticking to its fringes. I said hello, with a quivering emotional tone. She pulled her seer's ball out from under a red velvet cloth. It looked alive, with prisms of colour and light bouncing over the heavily-curtained caravan window.

Gypsy Leigh leapt into an unstoppable mystic diatribe without taking a single breath, proving to be a challenge for me to take it all in at once. "The minute I saw you, I felt your overwhelming grief, you lost a baby, I am so very sorry this happened to you. But this has indeed happened to you for a big reason. A huge reason, wow, you will go on and help many in your quest for answers and completion." Somehow, I already knew this. I felt I had dreamt it somewhere since Molly had died, but I could not place where or how. She continued at a faster pace. "However, I must tell you something amazing, truly amazing, when your age turns into its fifth decade, you will have another baby, oh my, yes there could be two babies." TWO? I gasped in disbelief! "You will be assisted by special professionals around you and in spirit. You have many alive and passed souls, who already want to thank you for the kind work you have done for them." I sat back, jaw to the floor; she must have meant my ambulance work.

"I see a big white building, it's tall, not wide, about five floors, in a city. Inside I see a very kind lady, not materially minded at all. Yes, her house is full of gifts from grateful others, cards, flowers, plants, photos of so many babies, which people have given to her. She treasures these items more than money. She is a baby specialist, who will guide you to finally becoming a mother to twins. Yes, I see needles, lots of needles, maybe IVF? She is not in America, but I see the letter A. Ok, no it is the other way, yes, in Europe; it is sweltering there. I can feel the heat, a biggish country; the letter A is strong. You will have assistance. What is your age now?"

"Forty-six," I said, feeling a fresh sprig of hope beginning to poke through my own toughened, concrete exterior, like morning glory flowering in a post-nuclear ghost town. "Take away your trauma lines, you do not look forty-six, do you smoke?" She asked. "No. I have never smoked." This was because I used to watch my parents lie to each other, then fight about the fact they had given up, when I knew neither of them had.

"I am feeling great sadness around your birth mother, she is not good to you, you must leave her be, as nothing will change with her now. This will bother you more as you become a mamma yourself. You are soon going to be standing tall and firm, with your husband by your side. But this will take hard work and much guts. Your husband, he will be a great strength for you." She briefly looked up from her ball. "We are not married yet," I replied, as I slowly twisted the single diamond engagement ring Brian had given to me, just a year before Molly had been conceived when he proposed inside the grounds of Windsor Castle. It fit snugly around my heartline finger, which possibly gave away our intentions. "Oh, but you are, you have both shared this experience of a spirit baby, that is a stronger bond than paper. He too needs to heal, he will do this in his own way, which is not your way, but the two of you will meet back in the middle somewhere. Do you have a dog?"

"No, we have never spoken about getting a dog." "You will be getting a dog, and this dog will show love and devotion, that is what dogs do. You will be moving house, before the new babies arrive. And mamma, watch for the number 22. It is significant to your journey. The crystal ball is fading." Her crystal ball did look dull like the batteries had died, and it needed a good clean. Even if all that was made up rubbish, she was well worth the morale boost.

We received a phone call from the hospital, informing us that Molly had returned from post mortem. I desperately needed time alone with her body. We were shown to a different room, it was not room eleven. Some other distraught parents were occupying that room, about to hold their dead baby for the first time. Once entering the new room, with every step towards her, I shifted deeper into foreign territory. I scanned the space for anything familiar to grab hold of, as the bereavement midwife showed me to the bed. I focused my attention on the outer weaving of Molly's Moses basket that rested on top. I looked in; she was still dead and wrapped up tight in a new yellow shawl. Slowly I unravelled her bare-naked body. It was a shock seeing raw stitching all bumpy and uneven across her chest bone, where they had opened her up with pinking shears and sewed her skin back together with a knitting needle. She felt heavier, solid, as the ice had frozen the blood in her veins. The nurse handed me the BA/BY grow as she left the room; it had been neatly ironed and sealed in a plastic zipper bag for hygienic purposes. I unzipped the bag and got it out to smell. It was soft to touch as, against my original wishes, it had been freshly laundered; this small item had been cleaned within an inch of its own life. They had washed her B'Earth-day clean away so that Molly's memory now smelt of Fairy.

Both feet wobbled while looking down at my silent daughter, Brian had to go out for a while leaving me alone in the new room with my naked, broken baby. She had become too frozen to even think about re-dressing. I could not bend her arms enough to get the chiffon dress I had bought her on. My tough exterior started to tremble, panic set in, I resorted to buzzing the bell for help. The bereavement nurse hurried in, explaining how we were both going to warm Molly up together. Gently, we picked Molly up from the Moses basket as if she were made of soft-paste porcelain, and calmly the nurse and my sweating fingertips started to rub her broken arm, then both flexed legs until some give returned. Once her cardigan and knitted trainer boots were on, her skull cap positioned to cover up her partly crushed head, Molly was transformed, she became more acceptable to the eye.

A few hours later, Brian joined me. He held his daughter in his arms as he sat quietly with her in an armchair. He wore his green NHS paramedics uniform, as after seeing her, he had booked a shift working on the first response car, in this same area of Berkshire. I did not argue with him about going to work, as this was his way of dealing with his loss. A little after lunch, it was finally time to let her go, to leave her to rest in her Moses basket, ready to go to the funeral home for her final journey. Another, uneasy kind of pain hit me hard in my belly, a wrenching ache of knowing full well that we will never hold her or see our baby ever again. Nor was it likely I could ever get pregnant without an almost biblical phenomenon. The specialist bereavement nurse nudged me away from my only child's body. I could not control my emotions a second longer; they flooded my entire system with all the love I felt for this tiny being. The sound of desperation screamed out an almighty primal squeal, like a small animal trapped in a snare in the woods.

This was our final goodbye, the very last time we would be able to see her, hold her, breathe in her sweetness. Both our hearts shattered into a million organic particles for Molly. Our little girl's final place of rest was across the road from the hospital, at the funeral home. The director took a bag containing all the items we wanted to be placed alongside her for her eventual departure to the Heavens, akin to the Balinese boy's cremation. There was not much to give. Unlike the fifteen-year-old Balinese boy, whose life had been full of activities, Molly had not lived her life for a single second. I thought back to his mother. I now wept for us both, as I felt complete respect for her. How can anyone cremate a teenager? Carefully chosen photos of myself, Brian, and her older brother Adam had been collected. I found various coins for wealth in her next life, some dried fruits and rice, so she never went hungry, poems her dad had written for her, a letter from us both saying how much we loved her; these were all we had to give. I found a Jim Reeves song that would open the Service of Remembrance. *'This world is not my home; I'm just passing through.'*

Steven, our hospital Chaplain, explained that it frequently happens that only a few people show up for a stillborn funeral. It is not rare, that on occasion, for even the parents not to attend, so we would not be judged if we decide it is all too much for us. There was no way Molly was going to be cremated on her own; we would both be there to the end. The funeral was held on 29th August 2013. Steven, the Chaplain, greeted us at the gates of the small, peaceful West Chapel in Caversham. He looked deep in thought as if planning what to say next, this man was an expert in what to say next in a crisis. Raising his eyebrows in complete surprise, he decided we needed to move everyone to the bigger chapel next door. He beckoned us both to turn around and look behind us. I feared that no one had shown up. How mistaken of me, as there were over a hundred friends, including members of three ambulance services, looking right at us! Everyone, from all walks of both our lives, stood shoulder to shoulder, metaphorically holding us both up to Heaven, so we could hand Molly over safely to the afterlife, so she would not suffer any unnecessary death-lag. No one from my family attended. Brian's older brother and his wife, and his younger sister came to offer their support.

The Funeral Director opened the passenger-side door of the hearse. Resting on the back seat was her tiny white coffin, which had two owl stickers which we peeled off her nursery wall. Brenda loved owls; I hoped Brenda was with Molly, feeding her a bottle and showing her videos of all my travel stories from my worldly adventures. We both stood at the main door of the bigger West Chapel; the chapel was packed. Even though all these people were here, I felt intensely alone. We were all uncomfortable, knowing everyone came that day for a baby who never took a single breath. I wanted to carry her in myself, but Brian looked at me with tears rolling down his face, saying in his most broken voice. "Claire, go sit down. I want to carry our daughter in, as you had carried her for forty long weeks. Now it is my turn to carry her to her final resting place. Please Claire, I need to do this." A guiding hand cushioned the small of my back, assisting me to my seat in the front row. I wanted to make a run for it, leaping into the furnace for departed darlings, so I could be with her for eternity. Bobby Vee said it all for us, in her final farewell song. *'Take good care of my baby.'*

40 WEEKS

I carried her for 40 weeks, I counted them
Each week heavier than the last
While the world cheered around me
I relished my new earthly mission
My first act of love
Within this breathing body
So heavy, cramped & unbreakable
Was her tiny body
I carried her to make things right
From conception to delivery
My womb her home
They waited, excited for the news
Until she let go of life

40 STEPS

I carried her for 40 steps, I counted them
Each step heavier than the last
While the world wept around me
I toiled with this earthly mission
My last and only act of love
In this mortal plane
So light, so small & fragile
Was that casket
Yet I gripped her so tight
From hearse to alter
My knuckles deathly white
They watched, bowed & broken
Until she embraced eternity.

SIXTEEN

And even the Gods betray us,
by the light of the bitter moon.

How do I continue life as a forty-six-year-old, redundant childless mother? Brian and I once enjoyed our days together, wandering around local picturesque towns, while we were expecting our miracle baby girl, but now it had become a living nightmare. All I saw were pregnant women, new mums, and kids everywhere. Trying on dresses was not a fun pastime anymore, especially since my tummy had changed shape so dramatically since the birth. Instead of internal organs crammed up to my bust, everything fleshy had dropped down to my pelvis. Our baby had gone, my uterus and breasts were unemployed. They were both in a headlock with mother nature, losing the war against rage and age, overpowered by gravid definition while gaining parturition defeat. I could not control myself a second longer when a random woman asked when I was due? I looked at her square in the eyes, "She died last week." Spoken as if Steven Spielberg had directed me, with his film crew capturing every moment in total location lockdown silence, a death certificate could be heard hitting the pavement below. Then, "CUT, that's a wrap folks, good job everybody!" Slowly, I pushed past her, as she was still working out which facial expression was most appropriate to use.

Shuffling along the busy High Street, trying to find my exodus, with every step forward, it was almost biblical as by-standers parted the way in front, so I could get through as it was briny deep of people. It was apparent that I was drowning from traumatic undertones. My face drained of colour. I was unkempt from the stress that my mind, body, and soul, did not know what to do anymore. Crushing Brian's hand, he led me to the other side of town to safety. At a loss himself, this mighty King of tribulation did everything in his power to protect his sorrowful Queen. Ahead appeared another dilemma, out of the far corner of my shame-filled eye, I spotted one of the phoney healers who I had visited many times. She had promised that her entire angelic team, including Archangels and Mother Mary herself, had confirmed that Molly did not have Down syndrome. This, in hindsight, was not her place to say, and in doing so this gave me false hope. The angel whisperer spotted me. I started to cry, thinking we would meet, maybe awkwardly embrace, but she purposely walked on by. I tried to believe she could not see my tears, as she left me to grieve in peace, because each time I thought about Molly, I broke down and cried. Please, angel healer, do not walk on by. I just cannot get over losing her. When I saw you last, I was two people, but now I am one person, with nothing else left inside, just let me swallow my pride. These are the tears and sadness she gave us when she suddenly died. Surprisingly, she was one of many weak people of spirit, who walked on by.

I broke down, my bare knees fell to the pavement below. I became positively hysterical while every bystander just stopped and stared at the public show of shame. Brian managed to get me to my feet and paced us both back to the car. He took me to our doctor, where I was given Zopiclone to calm me down. I went straight to bed, hoping I would not ever wake up. But I did, unable to breathe. My uvula had swollen, it hung low down the back of my throat like an infected scrotum. I had an allergic reaction to a nonbenzodiazepine hypnotic agent. Brian rushed me to the hospital, where I was given antihistamines and hydrocortisone steroid.

My body had spoken the only way it knew, by giving me pain in my throat. It said very clearly, no drugs. I swore to myself from that day forward, like all the other times in my life where I sank below the reasoning of depression, that I needed to get through this grief unaffected by suppressants. I was feeling my loss at its deepest possible levels, tiptoeing barefoot through its turbid shallowness, going deeper and deeper into its pain, submerging beneath its murky depths, there were no rubber life rings nearby. My transfixed expression held the assumption that I was locked inside my own, brown study of thought. Stodgy, comfort-sweet foods were the only remaining undetectable vice I had left. I was already the size of a semi-detached house; surely, no one would notice if I became a small estate. Thus, I began in earnest to fill the empty void in my abandoned tummy with food. My baby had gone, completely gone. I truly missed the heartburn, swollen ankles, and cramped knees. I missed the excitement of seeing her on a scan, which was the only time we saw her alive. I missed talking about our plans for her arrival. I was a redundant woman, whose breasts had stopped producing milk but had continued to leak, aching to feed the baby I should have had, who now sits inside a small white box by my bedside. I wanted to feed a hungry mouth, so I fed my own.

Her nursery became a place of stillness, a private place where I cried alone. I metaphorically kept her inside me, fed and watered. I talked aloud, so the spirit world could hear me being a caring and loving mother to my spirit child. I soaked her in the bath, with the rubber ducks that people had sent as gifts before she was born asleep. I chatted to her while washing up, explaining how to rinse glass properly. I mindfully walked alongside her in the parks, hurrying past the swings and roundabouts where living children played. Daily I asked for a sign that she was OK. I noticed every subtle change in the house, questioning if she might have moved things around to tell me she was present. I listened carefully to every conversation in the street, in case someone mentioned her name, continuing my search for her ghost, looking, listening, wanting to believe. The spirit of our daughter dined with me, she drove in the car next to me and crawled into bed beside me where I held on to her yellow shawl, given as a gift from her biology trip to the coroner. I hated myself. I loathed my body, wearing layers of oversized mourning black to cover up my shame. I forbade Brian, the man I dearly loved to go near me. Thanks to a T-total approach, I felt every single moment of my aching loss.

We received her post mortem report. Our daughter was found to be a moderately macerated female infant, with a degree of brachycephaly of the head, bilateral flexed hips, and a broken right shoulder, possibly all due to her difficult birth. Cytogenetics showed she did have chromosome 21 Down syndrome. Crown to heel, she was 46.7 cm, weighing in at 7.5 lbs. Apart from that, there was no evidence of cardiac or any other abnormalities, every organ had been dissected and analysed (which made grim reading), and it was concluded that her cause of death was, in fact, 'Inconclusive.'

One name I kept hearing was Vince Fuller; he was said to be the UK's only psychic surgeon. Psychic surgery creates the oddest sensations, since the practitioner, who is not medically trained, can somehow rummage around inside the body without ever cutting the skin open. This resembled what Linnet Kerr had done in Guatemala on my travels. I had nothing left to lose. Four weeks after we cremated Molly, I was sitting comfortably upon a plump, purple velvet cushion in his therapy room. His eyes were as clear as the Bora Bora sea. I felt an instant rapport between us, along with an odd tingling feeling in my right hand.

"Oh Claire, I am so sorry for your loss. I am not normally a psychic as such, but I specialise in psychic surgery, and I have a message for you. I am seeing a grandmother, who is the guardian of a little girl, not a baby, but she is around five years old. With long legs and she is wearing a sweet white dress, and cheeky with it!" A five-year-old? Something connected as my right hand tingled, as this was my vision of her when I went somewhere like Heaven during childbirth. Yes, this confirms that I did see her!

"This is certainly your daughter Molly. She is standing at your right side, holding your hand. Molly wants you to know that she was not meant to come to this world. She only needed to experience utero stages. There was a soul agreement between you all, including Brian. The reason this happened to you was so you could experience the emotional depths of pregnancy, motherhood. It was not a given that you would be a mother at all. Still, you have worked very hard since early childhood, overcoming many issues going back lifetimes. You tried most things and took many risks to become a better person, going outside all comfort zones, so your path of destiny changed recently. Does this resonate with you at all?" It did, in more ways than he would ever know.

"Molly came to break your fears of parenthood and childbirth; your ankle injury at work was to slow you down, so she could come in. Her purpose was to help you truly feel the depths of maternal love for your own child. There is no other love as powerful as this. You are her Earth mother; and you will experience motherhood again." Would this have not made my fears worse? "I will experience motherhood? But she is not here anymore, I have no physical child to take care of."

"On the contrary Claire, you are every bit a mother, her mother, and you will be again." I will be again, what does he mean by this? I am too old, but then again Don José and Gypsy Leigh also indicated this. "Molly, behave yourself! Jeez, she is so naughty. She wants you to know that between two and three years from now, this will all make sense. You and Brian have much work to do, that is all I can tell you right now. Shall we get you up on the bed and ready for your treatment? I work through spirit. I have a team of spirit doctors who may speak to you while work is being done, they will be showing me where in your body, you need assistance. I am not here to diagnose. But I can help to fix things, to some extent, do you understand?"

"Yes, perfectly." I sensed something genuine about this man, everything he had just described somehow rang true. I removed my shoes, got up on the treatment bed, and lay face down, fully clothed. He asked permission to touch my bare skin from the back, I agreed. The feeling through his feather-like fingers was a mild, natural sedative which created a light-headed and dizzy state of calm. Pins and needles plagued my right hand. His breathing changed, then his voice became more profound, clearer. Healing hands darted in every direction all over my back with turbo speed, dipping right into my lower back. With a sprinkle of tap water on a cotton bud, he continued to work his magic, as if he was using real metal surgical utensils, which he was not. A voice boomed, he introduced himself. "MY NAME IS CHARLES. HOW ARE YOU TODAY?" I jumped. "Well, I am doing my best, thank you, Charles."

"Good to hear. Molly is well, she is holding your right hand. I need to explain that our vehicle here with us today, Vince, took four attempts before he found the right mother, physical body, timeline, and environment to be born into, so he could later in his life work with spirit.

His fourth mother completed his birth plan, since which, his life has not been an easy journey. The other mothers all lost their babies, which was him every time. We are very sorry this happened to you, but you were chosen for the job." This spirit was very strong, very commanding. I sensed a force field around me. "I have fixed a slight tear in your bladder, nothing serious, and reconfigured your uterus, so you should bleed shortly. There is a lot of emotional backlog; your guilt and grief are blocking your heart line. This needs assistance in being cleared, as you have a lot of work to do and this could compromise future, vital timelines." Charles spoke with a beautiful, eloquent English accent.

"What work?" I asked, as my right hand tingled more. Fully aware that Molly was holding it tighter, I tried squinting to see her, then squeezing her back, but my nails dug into my own hand. "You will know in time. I am going to bring this session to a close, it has been delightful meeting you." He started to sew me up, using Vince's clever fingers, cotton buds and thin air. "Charles, thank you for helping me today." I felt strangely calm. "IT IS A HUGE PLEASURE, MY DEAR, MOLLY LOVES YOU, KEEP ALERT, AND NEVER GIVE UP."

I could see Vince's feet through the face hole of the treatment bed, as they both stepped away, then he sat himself down on the chair behind. His breathing returned to normal; he was back in the room. My first menstrual cycle came two days later. I had half expected menopause; this proved that life continues, and maybe I was not as old as I thought. I should have felt a lot sadder than I was, but Charles had done something unexplainable to alleviate any negative thinking, which was a good start. It was all still in there somewhere, but for now, I had been cleared, without the aid of anything prescribed or toxic, just a bit of kookiness.

The rented house, with its vaulted glass roof and painful memories of Molly growing from second to the third trimester, used to be full of activity, friends coming and going. This stopped after Molly died. Feeling alone yet at one with each other, Brian and I decided to get married. The estate agent phoned the Friday before our Monday wedding, bluntly informing us our landlord was selling. They were giving us two months to find somewhere else, even though we had just signed a second twelve-month contract, only later did I find out this was against the law to turf us out like this, but we were not thinking straight. I explained what had recently happened with Molly dying, and our wedding in three days. "Congratulations, and at the same time I am so sorry for your loss, that sounds bloody awful. So, can we get the photographer round while you are on honeymoon?" They did not care that I was borderline broken or that Brian was so close to breaking. We were near beggared financially, due to getting married, which we thought would help fix our fragmented relationship. Spiritually, mentally, physically, and emotionally, in all honesty, we were all-round bankrupt. We were pitiable and unfixable tenants who like the slaves to society that we are, we continued to pay our rent on time, in the hope of reaching a personal breakthrough of some kind.

Our April wedding day was on a Monday. I wanted this opportunity to send a clear message that we were still together and healing, which was a big fat lie. There was no obsession with thinness to get into a petite designer dress. My friend Lisa back from Lincoln Art College days, had created the most spectacular wedding dress, with a strong Dior feel to its design. We used lengths of silver duchess satin, this stylishly hauled itself over every redundant curve, thus firmly holding in all those bits that unnaturally rolled downwards after childbirth.

Molly should have been our bridesmaid, dressed up in a little white chiffon dress, just like the one she wore when cremated. After thirty years of great friendship, Michael, my King's Cross neighbour, had over the years been crowned as my second dad, and he proudly gave me away. This is when I realised that a life time of nurture from a dear friend overrode nature. The entire event had been designed with meticulous detailing solely by myself, which my former art teacher and saviour Mr Hull, was proud to be part of that day. Of course, I had to use the tarot as a thread for decorative table placements and in individual, good fortune favour bags. In keeping with the tarot theme, my friend Paula entranced all our guests with her weird and wonderful cards and ominous predictions. She laid out a spread for me.

"Mrs Mear, congratulations my dear friend, you know I see you are going to move house, my goodness it looks like twice; this first house will be very temporary, the second house is in about a year." The thought of moving house again was already daunting, let alone twice more. "Hey sister, don't you be feeling gloomy now, you just got married, and Brian is so lovely, he is perfect for you!" I knew this, but we had many issues still to overcome, none of this had been easy; it would have been easier to break up and never speak to each other again. "Well, right, this second house will be a real home for a long while. Something important will happen there, know that it is your destiny! Oh my." Paula looked up from the cards into my eyes; tears were teetering along her eye line. "Clairey, I can see a baby. Yes! I see you giving birth to a baby just after your fiftieth birthday." Paula said, with such excitement. "What, seriously? A baby, at fifty, that is three years from now! You know, I keep hearing this Paula." I could not believe this had been told to me again. "I kid you not, I see it. Just after your fiftieth, you are giving birth to a healthy baby. Gosh, look at these cards, this is insane."

"This baby has certainly chosen you as its parents." Paula was adamant; this would happen. "Healthy you say, there will be nothing wrong with it, this time? And just the one baby?" I asked to make sure no twins were coming. "Yes, I believe so, just the one."

SEVENTEEN

Scars upon open wounds, blister, and weep.

Two months to the day after my becoming Mrs Mear, we left the Oxfordshire house with its torturous sunroof and mixed feelings. Ceremoniously, I cleaned away all remaining memories of Molly or of us ever being there. Closing the door for the final time, with a twist of heart, I felt unable to let go of the fat part of the backdoor key, as it resisted release inside the lock. This house was where she grew, where I had been the happiest, and this is where she died. Our new address was always just a house in which to breathe, survive and sleep, we did not enjoy a second of it. It was small, cramped and overpriced for what it was. Oddly, as predicted by Gypsy Leigh, a new puppy found us. He was a German Shorthaired Pointer, we named him Mr Blue. The date of his homecoming, ironically, fell on the 12th of August 2014, Molly's first birthday. He was Molly's unique gift to us. It was an overwhelmingly emotional time to be bringing a puppy home, and I am sure his acute canine instincts picked that up. His beautiful presence soon fit right into our lives, as he began to heal us both by giving us something to get up for every day.

An image came to mind one restless night, of the IVF lady who Brian and I had conveyed a week after Molly died, to the same maternity ward where I too gave birth.

I had never thought about In Vitro Fertilization before that day. That patient of ours, in her moment of loss, showed me something special, it needed discussing. An appointment had been booked at a well-known clinic in lower Harley Street, London. Once inside, the clinic seemed chaotic, cold, and unwelcoming, it was nothing like what Gypsy Leigh saw in her crystal ball. We sat in the waiting room, with anxious ladies wearing boutique clothing, tensely clutching Hermes Birkins, waiting on plush velvet sofas. I wondered if all the money in the world could guarantee a successful pregnancy and a healthy baby at the end?

The doctor called us into his clinic; he was African and tough to understand. Brian and I had many dealings with people from all over the world, but he was something else. His office looked temporary as if he could wipe everything off his desk into an attaché briefcase in one go. He asked about our medical history, including whether our parents had any genetic issues, of course, I did not know. He read my pulse and blood pressure with a cheap battery-operated machine, purchased from a supermarket pharmacy. Noting down his findings and thoughts with a blue chewed up biro, I personally cannot stand blue ink, especially written on a scrappy sheet of notepaper. "I am forty-eight, so I need to know, do you seriously believe we have a slight slither of a chance, Doctor?" I asked, looking him in his slightly bloodshot eyes. "Yes, madam, every chance. We need internal, then blood, urine, sperms, let us go." He directed us into an examination room, with a female nurse present. The doctor inserted a transvaginal ultrasound; his screen looked cheap as it hissed black and fuzzy non-readable images. "Yes, see, you are excellent to have baby." He smiled, and that was it. Something did not feel right about any of this. "Hold on one minute; neither of us can see anything on that screen; will I be able to use my own eggs or will I need a donor; how do you know if I can carry to full term or not; how will this all work?" My interrogative questioning was verging on chief inspector standards at a crime scene. "We do plenty tests, no problem madam, the price list in the welcome pack." Casually glancing through the price list, I winced. "Can I ask how much it will cost to have one baby?"

"Well madam this wholly depends on variations, every one different, but it will be approximately thirty thousand, give or take." My gut instincts, along with our current combined bank balances, To Keep Watch and my new entourage of seventy-six Mayan spirit guides, opened the front swing doors and said to run! Brian was supposed to do a sperm test as we waited. He could not; this was not his fault, as the expensive-looking clinic was a false hope-baby-mirage with no love in it. No thank you cards, no flowers, no photos of miracle babies, the atmosphere oozed silent trustees and capital but lacked heart and soul. The final straw was meeting the nurse, who had already matched us up to a possible donor, although she knew nothing about us at this point. She showed us a book with hundreds of plastic sleeves. Each sleeve listing ten potential donors, all of them sounded too good to be true, with doctoral degrees in sciences, literature, art, space travel and levitation. They were of every nationality, British, European, Mongolian, and even Guatemalan which I quite fancied, a wise Mayan soul child. As we were leaving, we had to settle the first bill, which in total came to £650. Apart from the internal and one urine dip test, no bloods were taken, and they tried to charge us for the sperm test Brian did not do. That was when I told them that we will not be back.

One night soon after, a vision came to mind. It showed us both applying to the council for fostering, but in the dream, I could not see any children, just a hospital. This sparked an idea, a secondary new plan, a possible move forward, hope prevailed again. Once being part of the care system, briefly fostered as a teenager, I knew very well the pitfalls of how it does not work with the wrong combination of people. Still, I believed we could be the right people for an assortment of displaced children who desperately needed a home. Our applications were sent to the correct departments. Within weeks, we attended the mandatory weekend courses, and the authorities naturally asked many intrusive and deeply personal questions.

"Do you think it is too soon to foster after losing Molly, it has only been a year since her death?" Good question. I lied by replying that I felt strongly that it was not soon enough, which I guess by proxy gave them their answer. "How would you deal with a difficult child?" Her inquisitive eyes locked into my trapped soul. "Well, I would talk to them, offer emotional support and lots of love, long walks in the park, treats and cuddles." I think I was getting into being a puppy owner than thinking through the realities of being a guardian to a traumatised child.

"What if they are angry teenage boys from ethnic, strict, religious backgrounds?" That one stumped me, but I knew that Brian could handle it, he was good with any kind of teenage lads as he had a son of his own and had been part of *The Boy's Brigade* since he was eleven. "What are your daily stress levels like, on a scale of one to ten, since her death?" Another interesting question. For which I massaged the truth a bit, trying to convince them that we hovered around a five, maybe a four on good days. The truth was, we were both still at ten going on eleven on regularly bad days. "How many good and bad days do you have?" Bloody Hell, we were in trouble! They could mind read; they were on to us. Every word spoken was challenged and noted, filed in reports, uploaded as data on systems, then analysed by social workers and heads of departments with psychology and criminology degrees.

To finalise the next stage, the authorities needed an in-depth medical, completed by our doctor. Most of this went well, until the urine dip tests; instantly, our doctor noticed traces of blood in Brian's sample. He commented that it was only slight traces, barely detectable and we were not to be worried, but he must get this checked out as soon as possible, or he would not be doing his job correctly. The doctor turned to me and asked about my fitness levels, as I was looking a bit less rotund than normal. Proudly, I showed him my funky new health and fitness app on my fantastic *LG-G4* smartphone, as I had been walking Mr Blue daily. It pinged up, proving that I had walked fifteen point six miles that week, and it was only Wednesday afternoon. The doctor pointed out that my body mass index was high. It usually takes a good year for a woman of my age to lose her baby fat when the baby is alive. Sadly, when the baby dies, it can, of course, take a lot longer. Since I had been wearing my veil of depression, like an Emirates fashion model on an Abu Dhabi catwalk, I refrained from telling him the whole truth about exactly how many salted caramel shortcakes I scoffed daily. So, he was satisfied I was doing well, for now, stating how country walks can help enormously with not only physical fitness but overall mental health and general well-being. He was delighted I had started to help myself, writing upon his notes that I had not, at any time, asked for any kind of prescription assistance to block out and dumb down my grief (obviously my description!) Especially since the Zopiclone incident.

Three weeks later, we received a copy of the medical reports. Not only had it been well written, but it was convincingly compassionate. So much so, I wanted to be fostered by us. Alongside his statement was a second cover letter, from the council's staff paediatrics medical advisor in fostering and adoption. She had, somehow, translated every word my thoughtful doctor had written into torturous, attacking Cardassian.

'Mrs Mear, is a forty-eight-year-old married lady, who works for the institute of health and care development.' I am sure she meant to say that I am a full-time, self-employed film unit medic, as I had no clue what her job description of me was. 'Mrs Mear has no living children; she had a full-term stillbirth in 2013, (let's twist that knife in a little deeper). Her GP describes that she has coped exceptionally well following this. She has never smoked and does not drink alcohol. Her BMI is 34.6, which is classed as obese. Obesity is a condition that can affect the health of the persons that they look after. Children placed with carers who are obese are more likely to become overweight or obese themselves. This is not a good influence for any potential child she may foster. Her body weight will be irresponsible in teaching any child about basic nutrition and healthy living.

However, there are no other significant health problems identified that would impair the applicant's ability to provide short or long-term care to a foster child.'

Say again? What the F...!

Brian's report was an even grimmer read. 'Mr Mear is a fifty-year-old, British, married paramedic man. When the GP examined him 'significant' blood had been detected in his urine; this was sent with urgency to the urology investigations.' I was sure our doctor mentioned 'traces' of blood, not 'significant.' 'He is undergoing cystoscopy and biopsy tests, where so far there also appears to be abnormal appearances of part of his bladder wall. There is a strong suspicion of transitional cell bladder cancer. If this turns out to be the case, then Mr Mear is in no position to foster children at this current time, while he undergoes treatment and recovers.'

They found two, stage three, malignant tumours in his bladder wall. Neuroscientists explain that, 'the body remembers the body holds the score.' It retains all our pain, and that corresponds to various organs.

The bladder itself corresponds with high emotions. I wondered where my cancers were hiding after a lifetime of disappointment? A year since losing our firstborn, we had both just about worked our way through the first stage of grief, that being of disbelief and shock. We were about to submerge ourselves into stage two, raw, bloody anger. Brian felt powerless, all he wanted to do was carry on protecting me. Still, of late, especially after my sessions with Vince and Charles the invisible doctor, where they had unexplainably taken a considerable chunk of my pain away, I was harder to read. Brian did not realise, at this stage of our relationship, that my overall coping mechanisms for trauma, loss and complete disappointment were a lot stronger than his.

Willpower, stamina, and all hope had finally depleted Brian's energy; his anger now suppressed deep within his muscles and bones; his fragile heart had sewn lockets of loss onto his sleeve. Brian's tired feet drifted higher above the surface of this terra, as he took flight and did not want to fight anymore. Stuck at the epicentre of indecision, his grief had found its new home. Cancer buried itself within his bladder like two hungry assassin bugs. He had operations to remove the tumours, which proved to be incredibly painful for weeks after. It took eight months of treatments before he was cancer-free. During this challenging year, we crammed in Brian's fiftieth birthday, which we barely celebrated. I fought my hardest to help Brian return to good health and his old self, but maybe a new Phoenix needed to emerge.

My original dream was nothing to do with us fostering; I believe it was Molly, inching us both forward to get medically checked before another disaster. If I had not had that dream, then applied for fostering, we would not have found these tumours; she had saved her daddy's life. Still, nothing seemed to go our way, we just existed. Making pale excuses not to go anywhere together, we seldom visited anyone and struggled to do anything together at all as newlyweds. I did not draw, write a single word, or take any photos. Divorce was inevitable, except no one had mentioned this in any psychic readings so far.

EIGHTEEN

When time slips through the grasp,
like the dream of a dying man.

After yet another long day, I found myself hidden in a restricted location, working as a film medic. I spent many hours watching grown men build a YT-1300 Corellian light freighter galactic fighter ship, (which was the original *Star Wars* Millennium Falcon). Leaving work for the day, driving along the London Orbital, I began to think about how my dad would have been proud to see me working on all three *Star Wars* films. Back in the seventies, my Dad took me to the cinema to watch the original films. Steadily driving at sixty miles per hour along the motorway, I had the oddest sensation, of a presence I had not felt since 1988. "What have I done?" It was strange, I was sure I could hear my dad's voice. "Yes, I am your father, yes, it is me, and you are driving Vauxhalls, this Astra is a good model. Remember that blue Cavalier, when you were small?"

"Astra's do not concern me, Dad. What is this, are you dead? Have I crashed the car?" I said aloud, trying not to swerve, even though I was the only one wearing a seatbelt, as I still had a body that could die. Thinking back, I recalled that Arthur did not believe in any of this spiritual mumbo jumbo when Rita harped on about it daily. "I am dead, yes. If I only knew the power of the light side back then, I feel more alive right this second than ever before." My goodness, after thirty years of silence, I am talking to my dead father while driving, tired and at speed. Was he trying to kill me? Admittingly I did all my best thinking in the car, so why not now. I must be losing my mind.

"My little Clairey, just this once can I look at you with my new understanding, you were right about me. Tell that wonderful husband, you were right." My father was telepathically communicating with me.

"You have a ridiculously strong Gatekeeper spirit guide; it has taken forever and a day to sort this meeting out with you." Arthur spoke into my mind with a gentle calm Norfolk accent. "I needed to see you, see how life had treated you, as we both treated you appallingly. I am so ashamed. There is much to talk to you about, Clairey, and mainly..." He stopped to gather his thoughts. "Mainly Clairey, I wish to apologise. So, on these grounds alone, your Gatekeeper agreed I could get my visitation pass, but we do not have long." Slowing down to forty miles per hour, trying to concentrate on the road, "I cannot speak right now." I said aloud, which I really could not. Shock paralysed my mouth tight shut, as I dealt with unexpected emotions and irate European juggernaut drivers, who think they own the slow inner lanes on the motorway. Compounding this surreal situation, the sun was setting in the West, which was directly in front of my vision, near blinding both eyes. "Just think what you want to say, Clairey, I can hear you. I have tagged along while you have been working on *Star Wars*. Never, in my wildest imagination, had I expected that of you. Life is weird, but I have to admit death is weirder." He gasped with a big, regretful sigh.

"Well, you never gave me a chance to be little Clairey, did you?" A rush of teen anger surfaced but quickly simmered down, remembering that I was now the adult, and this whole carpool event was far beyond any adjectives. Still, now I was able to control myself with more manageable, grown-up emotions. "I have been with you all day today; it's inspiring observing you with so many types of people, including some famous aliens there I see."

"I am finally being paid more than beans to do it, Dad." I said with an air of triumph. After all these years of being highly criticised via the tenuous small-town drums of home, I had done well entirely off my own back. "Yes, you are right, and I am sorry I said that to you. It was incredibly arrogant, short-sighted, and narrow-minded of me. But you know what, I have been shown a film of sorts, inside screen three, my mind's eye, like a memory playback thing, no gadgets, it is very odd to describe. It was a little time after passing. I never believed there was anything after death, but there is a whole new reality going on here."

"Dad, I find your new trust in faith delightful!" I snuck that one in there.

"I found myself in a rather strange, after-world. Who knew there was anything beyond that miserable life I just left? To be honest, I wish I died years ago now." Since I can remember, I wished this for him too. "I was with you last week when you were filming at that airstrip, you know, where they made a tropical beach scene out of a concrete runway. Just incredible, to see my firstborn irrigating sand from a Storm Trooper's eyes!"

"I remember that day; you did cross my mind, you could say that I felt your presence, whooooaahhh!" I hollered, as I was always the clown, but now I was fast becoming the ringmaster. "You still have good humour, after all that pain we made you suffer. I have missed you." I did not know what or how I felt at that moment. "You know, we can tap into everything that has ever happened. I just had to think of you, and everything came into my vision. I said a date, and there you were on that date, doing stuff, amazing stuff, travelling the world, and Kylie, my oh my, you had a career in the music business after all. God damn it, Clairey, your living dad was an idiot."

"Do you even know who Kylie is, as she was not your kind of music at all?" How tables are turning. "Everyone in the Galaxy knows who Kylie is." It felt as if Arthur, my father, was very proud. "When did you pass away, and what with; did it hurt; were you scared? Was Rita there, did she help you at all, was she kind?" I was not taking any notice of the road ahead; this was becoming dangerous, worse than hands-free, which this kind of was. "I am not sure, but I have no pain now. I think I had a lot of pain when I was alive, unimaginable pain on all levels, mainly created by fear. When did I die? I simply do not recall, as there is no time here."

"Dad, please tell me everything about dying." This was better than Talk Radio.

"Let me think. I believed, all my life, that there was no afterlife, even with your mother costing me a small fortune, doing all that kooky stuff every week at the Spiritualist Church, which kept her occupied and happy. No, we did not agree on this. I am ashamed to admit that I have done a few people over in my lifetime, I have not made the best choices either, and I was a bit of a business rogue. So, I thought to myself, if an afterlife exists, it may all catch up with me there. Physically, I had not been well for a while. As I lay in bed, I felt a crushing sensation in my chest, followed by a loud snapping above my head. Then, it all went silent, no heart beating, no Venus returning, no breathing. It felt odd not to breathe. There were no worries of any kind, worry had left my body. I really was a dead man surrounded by my own fear. Oh, and no Saint Peter or golden pearly gates either. My spirit or soul whatever it is called, felt stuck inside that redundant dead body for a good while." I was curious if he could still hear anything, like seconds before being unconscious? He replied before I finished that thought. "There were very gentle muffled noises in the room, which I could hear like I was inside a closed box. Your mother was, of course, there. I did not hear her crying as I laid in a single bed, too damn afraid to move or to go anywhere. It was not clear what to do with my old self next. After a time, two exit eagles came to assist me."

What did he just say? "Eagles, don't you mean angels?" I double-checked, maybe I was not hearing him right. "Yes, eagles, they were the most exquisite birds of prey, that telepathically told me to follow them. They helped me up with their beaks and out of my old tired body, and I flew with them, up and up and up into the most incredible, warm light. We stopped just before we reached the source. They instructed me to rest a little while and think about the life I had just lived, no judge, no jury. Now, here I am with you, kind of back on Earth with no body, gosh satire right there! But I had to find you, you were my firstborn and first thought. I need your forgiveness in order to move forward." His words sunk into the pits of my stomach, a place where a lot of primal screaming had once evolved.

"So, have you seen anything to do with my life?" Worried, as I winced for a bit with all the crazy stuff that parents should not see like shoplifting from school days and partying in clubs and intimacy with partners, Eek! "Hahaha, well, most things clean yes, but a lot of it is private, they have a privacy law and data protection here too, so your Gatekeeper refused those kinds of viewings. Look, you did not have the best start in life, I was not the greatest male role model. I was weak." I was glad he finally admitted this.

"You always had a huge heart and incredible forward vision. Since you could first talk, you used to come out with so much stuff that we had no clue where you picked any of it up from. Then there was that answer phone you bought me for Christmas, well, I was so touched, in the end, I left it at work, so business people knew I was firmly engaged in the twenty-first century. All thanks to my busy, creative daughter living and working in London, dressing pop stars all by herself." "Oh yes, I remember, that time was followed by a nasty badly typed letter from you all, sisters included, telling me to sod right off! I did not fit into your vision of perfect family life, but we had no family life. Oh yes, you were very, very, proud!" I could not see my dad, but I could feel him. He felt calmer, softer, repentant, there was no arguments on any level.

"I am sorry I did not give you a chance; I did not support you or protect you from the world. Maybe, I was also protecting you from the both of us too. A lot needs to be discussed, there is so much you do not know. But what I can say to you is this, you have always been a good kid at heart, it was all our fault. If your mother could be turned, she would have been a powerful ally, alas this was not to be. We were the grown-ups behaving like kids. I speak only for myself; I am very sorry." I felt his remorse deep inside my heart. "Your Gatekeeper is giving me the nod; he is pulling me back; One day, you will be a wonderful parent, remember this. I am looking forward to meeting your beautiful daughter, Molly. I hear she is a delight, just like you were as a small child. And I am going to give our Brenda a big hug when I finally see her again, especially for looking after you all these years." I knew Brenda would be ecstatic about that. "Please thank your Michael for being such a support and stepping in as a second dad to you, I look forward to shaking his hand one day. Maybe, our bad parenting worked in the end. Your childhood, well, you were so vulnerable but tough at the same time; alas, it is what it is, and it has made you who you are now. Still, no excuses for not being around for you later in life."

I phoned his local registry, where I had to purchase a death certificate, for ten pounds, to obtain any further details. He had died peacefully at home, fourteen days before our carpool chat, in November 2014. He was eighty-three and had passed from rectal carcinoma. I cried my eyes out, realising that as he was the biggest pain in my backside for all these years, then he goes and dies from being it. I had not known him when he was alive, but I was feeling his loss on every level. My sad parents stayed together all these years, with no interaction with me or my sisters in the end. What an unhappy marriage. The death certificate said, witnessed by his wife Rita, her occupation retired 'typist,' which made me cry with laughter. Rita had not notified anyone of his death, he just slipped away. I sent her a condolence card that I had made myself; he was my dad, after all. I later heard this spooked her to the core, she was baffled as to how I knew. Rita did not respond, but she did not return to sender either, some progress maybe.

NINETEEN

My fingers are missing.
They lie in the lion's mouth.

I had reached the maximum bodyweight my circulatory system had ever had to deal with, unaided by pills, shocks, or stents. Thirty-one long, tiresome months being a childless mother. We had endured Molly's first and second birthday, two painful Mother's Days, a couple of sorrowful Father's Days. Every Christmas the decorations stayed in the attic. The glum, repetitive celebrations of another New Year with no baby growing up reaching her milestones, were painful. Molly should have been two years away from turning five. The five-year-old little girl that Vince, the Psychic Surgeon, swore he saw in the spirit world. The same five-year-old Molly who, oddly, I too had resonated with, as I had seen her in my night dreams. On the 10th of every August, we relived her death, and on the 11th the now-familiar total memory loss. The 12th day was her B(earth)day. The 13th, letting her go to post mortem. Her funeral had been on the 29th. Every moment of August dissected, then broken down into unfathomable pieces of what ifs on the days in between, which repeated year after year. I tried so hard to locate her within the spirit world; why had I not seen nor felt her of late, where had she gone, was she already re-born somewhere else? Why had she left us so near to her birth, was she ever in her body at all, was she ever anyone?

Being a Guatemalan Water Path Shamaness, made no difference to my understanding of, nor the coping of her death. There was still nothing that made any sense, in dream time, the nightmares and darkness continued. I needed to step away from this current fiction before I wrote its sequel. Nearly three years later, my ovaries will be receiving congratulatory letters from the Queen. My late father's accounts of Heaven sounded inviting. Life, as Claire was a struggle, passing through into the next life, seemed the better option. Vince's good work was fading. After my forty-ninth birthday, my morale plummeted to its lowest ebb, as I went on alone with my internal grief-odometer subtly pushing 'code red.' I barely spoke to Brian during this period; everything he did just annoyed me. We avoided each other, even sleeping separately. He went to his rock gigs, and I did nothing, apart from work seven days a week on yet another exciting blockbuster film, where I was bored out of my head. Everything and everyone around us became a noise. Hibernating in bed alone every night, I prayed to the double-crossing scheming God, who took our baby away, unaware that I had reached the bargaining stages of grief.

"Hey! All you so called Gods and Goddesses within this Multiverse dimension. Not needing to remind any of you what you did to us, you bloody well broke each of us in two; and you flipping well held on to our Molly at the very last minute. HOW CAN YOU DO THIS? I need help! I am not sure who else to pray to right now, no one can bear to listen, so you will have to do. I do not need your pity, as I know you do not do mercy, it is a silly human thing, but please just point me in the right direction. Maybe one of my seventy-six shamanic guides could show up and help in my quest to reclaim who the Hell I am? I am formally asking for help. I have no idea where I am going, or if I want to be married anymore."

"I will do whatever you wish me to do with two conditions. I will never go to a church, or convert to any organised religions, not in this lifetime if I can help it. My faith and belief in spirit have been enough until now, it just needs reclaiming and tweaking. I need my life back. I deserve a family of my own, a child of my own, which right now will be the biggest miracle next to the Virgin Mary's experience into kinship. I will leave it with anyone up there who is listening. Molly, are you listening to your mum? Please give me a sign, any signs you are real. Dad, please come back and talk to me, preferably while I am stationary at home. AMEN. Forgive me for the AMEN part, it does make me sound a bit of a fraud. But I am desperate."

At forty-nine years and twelve days old, depression roared up through clogged arteries. The 'how is Claire social media devotees' had swiftly moved on to the next online drama, and a generous fraction of them were never heard from again. By now, most of my loyal friends understood I was one of life's survivors, forever parading as the victor, not as a victim. The strong female outer personality of Claire was fierce, all thanks to the wonderful University of Disappointment which, unfortunately, was my hereditary birth-right during this progeny of an existence. This included within its curriculum, rejection, activities on busting the human fear module, understanding the concepts of love, along with handling the arts and crafts of abuses since kindergarten. They knew Claire was always fine in a crisis, because this version of Claire, oddly now a London trained ambulance medic who saves lives, never asks for help. She helps others before herself and never gives up on anything, to ensure she will not hear her parents ever mutter that line, 'we told you so!'

Brian's purpose in this bromidic marriage-of-doom was to make sure his wife was fine. By now, she was used to showing the world that, on the outside, she was rich in colour and detailed in order, but he knew underneath she left a discontinuous mess of tangled emotions and hurt. Brian's job and priorities in this marriage were, to make sure his baroque tapestry of a wife had a weekly bunch of colourful flowers, that all meals were freshly cooked from scratch, and the rent paid. He was determined to make sure his wife, the mother of his departed daughter, was fine. This was all at the cost of his own fineness, as Brian, Father of Molly, and recent cancer survivor, was not fine at all. He was also just as wretchedly unfine as his wife.

The darkened skies looked ominous, as Saturn and Neptune screamed at the moon, which was in forbidden transit. Just as Mars, Uranus and Pluto were busy fighting and combusting in this our fine galaxy, it looked a lot like Armageddon. No amount of shamanic rituals or chanting could stop the romantic fantasy of giving up. My thoughts were to just get it all over with, to devour the remaining box of zopiclone (left from my first public breakdown), in the hope my entire body would blow up like a pufferfish. Then to somehow, spontaneously combust on the spot, leaving my shoes intact but slightly singed with a single black scorch mark on the concrete below. Instead, taking a minute to think things through, I sat alone, eyes momentarily closed, wondering what to do next? It was a school night, as both ears were saturated by the melancholic Coronation Street trumpet solo, which had comforted most of Great Britain since my early childhood.

Swiping through Facebook with spiteful fingers upon the protected glass of my kindle, my urge was a keen one, to leave ridiculous, random, borderline rude comments on people's pointless posts about their fabulously fake lives. I was sitting alone with my broken bare-self, clothed only with fabric cut from a yard's length of desperation, awaiting entry into Hell's own fiery salvage yard for discontinued human life.

No, wait! Someone noticed! Almost immediately, the phone rang; it was not a text, email, Skype or What's App, the phone actually rang. Since no one calls anyone these days, it made me jump. I had known Catherine for over thirty years, back in the days of *Blitz* magazine and Kylie, she had loaned me the *Red or Dead* shoes that Kylie wore. These were the same days when tragic stories, such as mine, were generally discussed on *Trisha*, every morning before *Richard and Judy*. "Are you alright?" Catherine inquired, as I had not seen her since Molly's funeral.

"Yes, I am alright, how are you?" Of course, this reply was the standard grey yarn I preferred to knit all my lies with these days. "You don't seem all right. I am reading some crap you are putting on Facebook. You're not all right, are you?" She asked, being the dutiful friend, I did not expect. "OK, you got me. I am not all right." The whole truth spurted out with the speed of an industrial weaving loom. Each word held tension, as I picked away at the realities of losing Molly. In one conversation, the nomadic tapestry I had spent a lifetime weaving, holding up in public, admired by the few not the many, had now been turned over for analysis. Its complex weaves and knots, hidden symbolism was now shredded and broken down into sample pieces by a good friend who understood the boundaries of fashion. I literally woke up shortly after, speaking aloud so I could hear myself. "This was not how my story would end! I was not going to be that sad, middle-aged woman with the late baby anymore."

My first steps into my baby-loss recovery were to:

1. Accept I was powerless; my life was the pits, whatever I did made no sense.

2. Begin to believe again; my faith was shattered; I am very broken. I needed to find out if there was some higher power either above, below or within,

that could help me through this blackness and shed some light.

3. Dare to surrender; as an abandoned child and now a trained medic, these two parts of me found it hard to push past pride and ask for help.

4. Trust that everything would fall into place; and that this one single, traumatic event would change me for the better, so I could end up helping others, through my own valuable experiences. This was as far as I got with my grief step programme.

After my heart-to-heart conversation on the phone with Catherine, on that miserable winter's night, she recommended I see her dear friend, who was a therapist. To jump-start my recovery, a decision was made to reduce the days I worked, this was the easiest part. Going from seven days a week down to six, letting go of Saturdays, as this was a special day for me to go into Brixton, London and see another Claire, also spelt with an I and E. Ms Claire DaBreo, was a five elements acupuncturist and therapist. Not long after my forty-ninth birthday, Claire D became my new therapist. I had never had a therapist in my life! We worked together very closely. She made me feel welcome and relaxed; she was easy to talk to and very funny, considering the circumstances we laughed a lot, which did not feel wrong at all. She spoke to me using simple, short sentences so that I could hear her through the deafening noise that is maternal silence. Grief itself has many volumes. Mine had, of late, been cranked up to number eleven, so they say in certain rock circles.

Five Elements acupuncture is very different from regular acupuncture. Claire D skillfully removed the truth from my clenched jaws, like a dentist steadily extracting an infected tooth, loosening the grip of grief from the grim tale which I had become. Buried words describing hidden feelings found their way up my oesophagus, squeezing a mishmash of syllables out through my voice box into the open air. They were freeing me from the dark moth-bitten cloak that had been wearing me down for the past three years. She worked out which meridian lines were blocked; and which ones were restricting movement forward. She felt her way around my depleted Ch'i lines, jump-starting this broken body along this energy highway.

Her trained, sensitive fingers always touched my skin, not letting me go like a blind person negotiating her way around the London Underground. She moved in close to smell me, inspecting my tongue, studying both eyes, observing how I stood up and sat down. She felt my skin, was it cold, damp, clammy or hot. Her needles stabbed pockets of blocked skin in precise, short, sharp bursts, into and then out of the most congested, stagnant areas. Venus was returning; blood began to flow freely around my circulatory system. I sat up straighter; my mind cleared itself, ready for new ideas. Sleep became a joy, my moods levelled, pitiful anger moved out, as the beginnings of self-love waited to move in. Incredibly, I began to feel more accepted. Claire D asked two simple questions about my weight. "Are you feeling hungry, or are you feeling empty?"

"Empty." I replied. The baby that was once inside me is not there anymore. "So, there is no need to fill it with food is there?" Claire D was right. "What is your goal for these sessions?" Good question, I pondered. "Brian and I have rebranded Mearfest, which is our rock festival charity event which raises money for special Hospices, Kids and Cancer charities. We will be using Molly's handprint as our new logo, raising money for the Willows stillbirth support group who provided room eleven at Royal Berkshire hospital." I had many reservations about being so public. It hurt every time we told our story.

"Claire this sounds amazing, well done both of you. It's hard to talk about such a loss so soon, let alone so publicly." Claire D's eyes widened, she looked excited. This was an initial triumph, as three years ago when Molly died, when there was no future at all, to today, where we now have a plan. I savoured her words. I explained further, "Brian's aim was to get fathers talking about their losses, through rock music. He felt there was no support for him throughout this experience, which was true. So, my goal is to be able to stand in front of three hundred paying guests at our next Mearfest charity event. Assuming we sell a single ticket, we would host this event on the 13th of August 2016, in the name of Molly Mear. That day would be three days after Molly died, and one day after she was born asleep, on her third birthday. "Well, let's get you centered and strong, ready to let go of the past and deal with each day as it comes." Claire D said with conviction and compassion.

During a windy but warm April, Sunday morning, Brian and I attended a memorial service for the sleeping babies of Royal Berkshire Hospital. Just before we went in, we met one of the still-mums, Alva, who had lost her son, Harrison, a few years before. She went on to have her miracle daughter, Ella, who was now three. Unexplainable emotions and excitement took over, seeing this little girl. She was a picture of beauty and perfect health, and somehow it gave me the hope I was looking for. Alva explained that she was an IVF baby created in Athens, Greece, and she understood that they helped couples to have a baby up to the age of fifty-one. This gave me at least three years of even more hope. I could not stop looking at Ella throughout the service, thinking about my tarot reading with Paula on our wedding day. I also contemplated Gypsy Leigh's prediction of two babies, and a hot place beginning with the letter A, could this be Athens? Shivers of insight tingled my face as if someone was holding me close, but could I dare to go through all this again, aged fifty?

I recited a moving poem at the Service of Remembrance; as new cries were audible from the recently bereaved. Their pain was all too familiar, as everyone attending had this tragedy in common. It is an extraordinary union that no one intends to sign up for a lifetime membership. For the first time after Molly's death, we both felt four calling-birds-of-grief leaps ahead of many people present that day. But we were still three steps behind the rest who had set up the Willows support group many years before. A few ladies went on to have rainbow babies, this is a healthy baby born after a miscarriage or stillbirth. Something had changed. Vince's voice was whispering in my head, reminding me that Molly promised within two to three years; this would all make sense. We were in that third year now, and suddenly ideas and new plans were emerging. Waking from a halcyon dream, the words "never give up," kept repeating in my head. I knew upon waking that morning that we would go down the IVF route.

Claire D, my incredible therapist, was also a respected fertility expert. I approached this new plan the following Saturday, in her Brixton therapy room. "We have much work to do," she announced. I was forty-nine; she passed no judgement. I had stopped working Fridays, Saturdays, Sundays and now Mondays, enjoying this my new three-day working week. We did, indeed, move house yet again, this time the rental house was 0.4 miles from Stoke Mandeville Hospital. Nestled snuggly within the more agreeable grief period of acceptance, I was finally able to stand back from my droll viewpoint. Looking in at where we were, and with a bit of bravery, self-confidence and focused determination from me, we could be heading to Athens.

The bigger picture began to shift in shape, starting with the corners and edges first. We had enough savings, from both of us working nearly seven days a week for three years. In July 2016 flights were booked to Athens in Greece, to have our first consultation with Serum, the IVF clinic. Penny welcomed us. Her clinic was, as predicted by Gypsy Leigh, a tall white building, not wide. Penny had an incredible motherly warmth about her; she felt like Mother Earth herself, who cared about results, not profits. The clinic was indeed warm as in welcoming, and not just the Greek summer humidity. It had been filled with thank you cards, along with photographs of all the babies they had created, safely brought into this world. We stayed in Athens for a week, while the clinic ran many tests. Brian's sperm had to be checked, his results came back three days later. "Mr Mear," the young nurse shouted out into the crowded reception area. "Yes, that's me." "Your sperms are 100%!" With that came a roar of applause from the British mixed and same-sex couples sitting in the adjacent waiting room.

Next came an internal check on my uterus. "Mmmm, this is not good. Claire, you have no viable blood supply." Penny said as she frowned at the monitor. "What do you mean?" I wanted to cry. "Look at this mass of fluffiness, looks like clouds, this thick stuff attached to your uterus, see here?" She prodded my uterus that had no blood supply beneath the bulging mass. "You have a lot of hyperplastic, which is covered with scar tissue; endometrial hyperplasia is defined as an abnormal thickness of the lining due to hormonal dysfunction. The main reason for scar tissue is chronic, asymptomatic, and unspecific uterine infections. It is a common finding that is recognised by many ladies." Penny continued. "This is not something that concerns us, but it affects implantation rates a lot, if untreated my dear, this means the fertilised egg will have nothing to attach itself to and grow, it will just die." I was sure the lower Harley Street overpriced IVF clinic had stated not six months before, that I was ready to go.

"This is not a big problem; we will send you for a hysteroscopy tomorrow at Athens Women's Hospital. You must come in the day after tomorrow with the DVD." Penny instructed, with complete authority, that things will be OK after this operation. A hysteroscopy is performed under general anaesthetic, it is an inspection through the cervix of the uterine wall, which is where the fertilised egg needs to latch onto to grow. This can detect benign growths, which then can be removed, performed by an endoscopy, accompanied by a small film crew, thankfully with no sound boom! The impressive award-winning DVD had clear images of fluffy womb clutter being cut away by the surgeon, like a champion sheep shearer at a farm show. "YES, this is very good now; the baby has a good home to grow, see?" She brought our attention back to the surgeon on the DVD pressing against the uterine wall, where squirts of blood were released. "Now, an excellent transfer can happen, you need to start these drugs, some anti-inflammatory and antibiotic tablets after your operation. Clexane injections to thin the blood, so not to suffer a clot. Cyclacur hormone tablets for enhancing progesterone, to help the placenta to grow. We were to have donor eggs as mine were not good. Penny knew who would do this for us. We would come back in seven weeks when we hoped there would be several fertilised eggs to transfer into me. God Bless Gypsy Leigh, Alva, Harrison, and Ella, who got us here.

TWENTY

Rekindle our lost dream,
igniting the fuel of shrouded hope.

July's focus was on physical health, emotional and mental wellbeing. Alongside daily injections, taking pills, focused disciplines, and spiritual mindfulness was a dash of hope. We were busy rebranding our little rock and metal festival, Mearfest. Four stone in weight had dropped off since February, thanks to the daily walking with Mr Blue. Of course, Claire D's needles supported all these other changes. Staying positive in mind was the only way this was ever going to work. I envisaged my stomach bursting with hope and not salted caramel cheesecakes, and my uterus full of a growing living baby with a healthy rich placenta.

Annually, the 10th of August is Molly's day of death, although the exact moment will never be known. This year felt different, there was no nagging soul-crushing guilt to continue my paranoia that I had somehow killed her. What had changed? On the 11th of August, again, no memory. Utilising this time wisely, we prepared for the inaugural Mearfest in Molly's name in London. Our first t-shirts had arrived that morning; her tiny handprint was the only tangible part of her left, now visible for the world to see on the outside, her handspan covering the metal community's giving hearts. All those acupuncture sessions had come to this; testing, if it worked, would commence in twenty-four hours. That night, an intense dream had me thrashing around. It was about Molly; she was telling me to let her go, showing me a white box and a wind chime.

2016 should have been Molly's third birthday. It had been usual for us to wake up in tears on the 12th of August. Except for this year, Brian and I woke up and talked about my dream, and instinctively knew what to do next. It was time to return the original white cardboard box that held her remaining ashes back to the crematorium in Caversham, Berkshire. We decided that it was the perfect time to let our baby girl's ashes go, scattering her into the elements, to set her spirit free. This was a liberating act; we ceased our grieving, understanding that our lost daughter will return in another form. This was something I had learnt a great deal about while travelling around Asia and reading lots of Rumi quotations. The Willows charity-sponsored a memorial garden within the crematorium, where, bending down, I looked at all the headstones of children lost at every age. Many graves had been abandoned, obscured by wild overgrown weeds, saplings, and grass. Hidden beneath were forgotten teddies, dumper trucks and my little pony's all left to bring comfort to the children of ghosts' past.

Later, it was explained that families and parents are more likely to split up after the death of a child, and move away to forget. No baby is ever forgotten. Part of me wished at this time that we had buried Molly so that we had somewhere to go to visit her, but my strong faith in the afterlife had taught me that spirit is with us wherever we go, I often wondered was her spirit ever in her body as it grew inside me? I wanted to drop to my knees, and with both empty hands begin to pull out the weeds from the same ground where a tiny human life was once buried. There was an assortment of wilting, decaying flowers wrapped in decorative, non-biodegradable cellophane and ribbons. Some smashed, unattended potted plants lay next to dirty soft toys, covered in powdery mildew, where white fuzzy spores leapt up to dance within the allotted playground of each plot.

The only living items were garden windmills, in hues of the rainbow, catching the light with sparkly glitter. Wood and metal wind chimes were held up on sticks, given movement by the summer air so broken cords and inharmonious melodies could ward off any malevolent spirit. My dream of wind chimes now rang true. We found a Silver Birch and knew this was where we should set her free. Timidly shaking the box, away from the tree so as not to damage it, we said a prayer. Brian took my photo just after her release. It was not until we got home that we saw cylindrical light orbs around my tummy. Was this some sort of a sign, was Molly now free? Or was this our new baby saying hello?

Saturday, the 13th of August was our first ever rock and metal event, in the name of our dear baby, Molly Mear. We held Mearfest at the Borderline in Central London. Leading up to this day, a few rival event organisers found it appropriate to mock us, saying both to our faces, and behind our backs, that the combination of stillbirth and rock music would never work. Regardless, every ticket had been sold, as were all our t-shirts. More importantly, we both managed to hold it together for the entire twelve-hour event, big thumbs up for five elements acupuncture and living more of a stress-free life. Our purpose was not for profit, but to raise money for the Willows and awareness of stillbirth and miscarriage.

At first, it was oddly bizarre, seeing our baby's handprint everywhere, as she proudly hung from a vast, white backdrop supporting every band playing live on stage. The same handprint was worn by most people in the room, though I had to admit that trying to enjoy this new wave of British heavy metal sound was going to take me more than nine months of therapy. There was no aggression, no circling mosh pits full of sweaty, long-haired headbangers, and no judgements. Together, we celebrated the life of Molly. A life that was, oddly, never lived, but here she was, holding the giving hearts of all those wearing her sweet little hand. That day we raised £6,884.99 for RBH & Willows Support group..

Three weeks later, my ovaries needed to be in ovulation. Even though we were not going to be using my old eggs, it was more about the timing of the donor and my own cycles. The twenty-something-year-old Greek Goddess of a donor (we will never know who she was), and my own forty-nine-year-old antiquity of a reproductive system, needed to be in perfect synchronicity. It was becoming more like an egg and spoon race, while running inside a hessian sack on school sports day, no pressure! An internal scan was required while we were still in England, to see if the lining of my womb was to the right thickness post-hysteroscopy, to be able to carry a baby to full term. I had no hocus-pocus power over this, apart from a lot of hypocritical praying to the God I had previously scathed with resentment. I relied on the hope that all those fertility drugs, acupuncture needles, and basal body temperature readings every morning, had been enough to get us over this next scary bridge made from fragile endometrium epithelial and mammalian layers.

The familiar waiting room in the London scan clinic, had mothers-to-be clutching onto their Michael Kors handbags, gold iPhones, and aching to hand over their Coutts credit cards. The receptionist sat behind a semi-circular desk, on the phone to a mother-to-be, trying to be discreet, but I heard every word. "So, I have good news and bad news for you today." This was sounding very familiar. "The good news is your baby does not have Trisomy 18." She paused as she prepared herself for the

191

jugular throttle, it brought back that day in March 2013, when we received the same good and bad news. "The bad news is your baby is 99% positive for Trisomy 21." She paused again, breathing in deeper while squinting one eye as we all heard hysterical crying on the other end of the phone line. I wanted to grab the office phone from her hand, to tell that mother-to-be to monitor all movements from thirty-seven weeks, and never to give up.

The scan measured my uterine wall as a thickness of 11.5 mm, this was a perfect measurement, everything had cleared up from my previous operation. Finally, this organ will hopefully enable me to carry a baby to full term. Many women fall at this hurdle, as anything below 4.5 mm will not sustain life. The following day, on the 18th of September 2016, we travelled to Athens for the second time, staying at the Polis Grand Hotel in the city centre, with magnificent Acropolis views from the rooftop garden. The clinic phoned that evening, explaining they had successfully harvested and fertilised five fresh Grade A eggs that day. We had five perfect blastocysts (which means 'sprout' in Greek), our five babies were currently one whole day old. The morning of the 22nd of September 2016, was day five of our blastocyst's life, confirming that I would be a little over fifty years and four months old when they are born, and the number 22 was right there. My mind rolled in reverse, this is precisely what Gypsy Leigh saw, 22 and twins! Paula, on the other hand, only ever saw one baby, but she did see the exact age I would be when I had my second baby. Don José said I was to be a mum, and Vince, the psychic surgeon, had spoken to Molly shortly after she had left us, implying that I was to be a mummy again. Even my dead dad said the same thing in our carpool journey along the London orbital.

This was finally happening to us. Precisely three years after Molly left us, in our second house after she died, we had indeed created a music festival in her name and new life. The lighting in the treatment room had been dimmed to cosy, warm, receptive levels. Both my legs were assisted up into stirrups and a modesty blanket hid Aladdin's cave. The quality and quantity of these eggs had Penny and her biologist in raptures. At the very last minute, it was decided that only two five-day-old babies would be transferred. "Ready to receive your two babies?" Penny asked with a big smile. I could see her cheeks rising and the corners of her mouth beaming clearly from behind her surgeon's mask. "Oh yes, we are," I said, as Brian crouched down beside me. A long catheter was inserted, two tiny white shooting stars launched into my forty-nine-year-old shipshape galaxy of a womb. With renewed hope, thanks to medical mirabilia and impending rainbow joy, we now had something extraordinary to look forward to.

TWENTY-ONE

Until your hand is in mine, the world stands still.
Nothing else matters and nothing else will.

Housekeeping had placed a bunch of beautiful flowers in our room, on the insistence of the manager Vassallis, who could not believe what we were doing. He felt honoured to have babies made in his hotel, that he knew of! Housekeeping also left plenty of shower gels and six extra pillows allowing ample comfort, so that both blastocysts could settle into their new environment. I prayed to the ancient in-vitro Gods of Athens, I was sure there was a Galaxy of them, as Greeks are world leaders in producing Gods and Goddesses, and this kind of fertility procedure. My request was simple, could they please latch onto a decent patch of cultivated blood supply, like tomato seeds in an allotment, and to feel right at home and snuggle within my warm cultivated womb. Brian became hunter-gatherer finding fresh chicken and Greek salads to keep us all nourished. We gave ourselves two whole days of complete rest, with box sets and steady walks through the Acropolis.

The anticipation officially started from the minute the babies had jumped from the catheter. The other three fresh fertilised Grade A eggs were put on ice, which is called embryo cryopreservation, just in case, it all went wrong. Fourteen days turned into a mini-millennium until it was finally the nail-biting time to rip open the pregnancy test. For me at forty-nine, and Brian at fifty-two years of age, what were we thinking? We half expected to be flying back to Athens to start the whole process again before Christmas. But at this stage, I needed to keep a super-positive mindset. From the moment we returned from Athens to Aylesbury, for the first two weeks I barely moved a muscle, to avoid knocking them both off their uterine perches. Fear of loss kept me observant of movement, like a Tai Chi master.

Three hundred and thirty-six-ish hours after transfer, the bedside clock inched its way past its October sunrise. The digital pregnancy test had been on standby for the last twenty years. At fifteen minutes past seven, the packaging was savaged, ready for the rest of our lives to begin. We both waited patiently for anything optimistic to happen, almost fearing the worst. The test started to shine its results, as it lit up with a positive, smiley face! Our babies were two weeks and five-days-old embryos. The sound of laughter echoed around the bathroom, followed by tears of joy and a lot of careful hugging. I truly loved my husband Brian, his unwavering devotion and love towards me, had, in turn, created something magical. A maternity miracle had happened to us for the second joyous time. To think I once turned him down!

Early morning, before dawn the first day of the sixth week, I began to spot. Panic raised both our blood pressures to critical. Remembering to breathe and calm my irrational mind, frantically we both googled, what does it mean when you are spotting? Am I losing a baby when bleeding? Is it normal to bleed so early on? These were somewhat stupid questions since we were both medics with forty years of frontline experience between us. We asked the GPS to drive us to the nearest scan clinic, as London was a bit too far away in an emergency. Thankfully we stumbled upon a wonderful clinic in

Marlow. The minute we walked through the door, we felt optimistic; the serene professional sonographer was the tonic to our mocktail. A transvaginal ultrasound projected the most precise images onto the flat screen fixed to the wall in front. She confirmed both babies had their own individual sacks and that they would not have been identical, but one embryo had gone. A dark empty shadow measured 31 by 2.5 mm, which was where baby one had given up, slipping away through the front door.

This was a chemical pregnancy, where an IVF baby dies very early on. Of course, there were mixed feelings about having twins. On the one hand, we would have to cope with two babies as fifty-year-olds, with no immediate family or friends living nearby to help. We had initially moved to Aylesbury as it was a central location to all the film studios where we both worked as medics, we had no clue we were going to have two babies at our age. I knew how difficult two babies could be, seeing the stress it caused my mother and me, as I grew up with younger twin sisters. On the other hand, as the babies grew older, they could keep each other company and not be an only child to geriatric parents. Then again, if this second baby dies, could I find the courage to go back to Athens and do the fertility drug cycle and transfer again?

The second baby was small for its gestational age. Still, more prominent than its twin's abandoned sac, it measured from crown to rump 2.8 mm, described as a single live foetal pole, which is the earliest stage of life. It had a head end and a tail and looked like a prawn jerking around within a single sack in the correct position. This embryo had a defined yolk sac, which gave it all its nourishment during the next stage of development; this part becomes the foetus around the eighth week, which is when it grows into its new body. It looked as if the foetal pole was carrying its heart on its back like a glowing living halo; its fast pulsations made our own hearts thrum. This baby was already ahead of the game, a fighter. The bleeding did not stop, so we returned to the clinic three days later to check if our little prawn was alive. Our miracle Rainbow had already grown to 4.1mm, with a robust foetal heart pulsation, but it was still too soon to hear the sounds. This was such a gift, to be able to see our baby so soon, in such a primitive form, it was smaller than a pea. The bleeding finally stopped later that day, although we realised, we had a long journey ahead. We were nowhere near the finishing line.

Anxiety took over before each scan appointment, this became routine. The dread of impending doom drove with us to every clinic appointment. This is a natural feeling after a full-term stillbirth. At no point, until this baby is here or until it became a healthy adult, could we relax. Experiencing my second early miscarriage was upsetting, so I needed to continue to think positive thoughts and keep this second baby alive. Every time we saw it kicking and spinning around on the 3D coloured screen, we could not help but run out of the clinic fist-pumping the air, screaming with delight. Somewhere within this decluttered, plumped up, semi-ancient cave of a uterus, our baby kept on growing to its perfect centile.

At eleven weeks and two days, we had another private scan. This time we could see two arms and legs and its stomach, its heartbeat could be heard for the first time at 168 bpm. We ordered another Harmony blood test, to determine if this baby had Down syndrome T21, T18 or T13. This time the egg was from a youthful donor, who had been genetically screened and tested for all these kinds of abnormalities. I had to keep myself locked within a positive mindset. The results were a definite 99.9% negative for Downs and all other chromosome conditions with a probability scale of less than 1/10,000 (0.01%) risk. For the first time in my life I ignored that 0.01%. Alongside the result was the baby's foetal sex, overjoyed we read the word female. We now stood firmly on the red of the bull's eye.

Twelve long weeks had passed since the transfer; the IVF drugs would be ending soon. They had served their purpose, the placenta was in place and working well, regularly giving our daughter everything she needed for a happy all-inclusive stay until check out sometime in June 2017. Her official nuchal scan confirmed all measurements had been read correctly by an NHS sonographer, who had no decorum at all. "Gosh, you are forty-nine years old, that is very late to be having a baby, is this your first?" He said with a surprised tone in his voice as if we were lifelong friends sharing some recent gossip over a latte! "Second actually, can you not read my notes?" Snapping back, naturally upset, as I was still raw and highly-sensitive from overripe hormones, general middle-age worries and the whole previous daughter number one experience. After that awkward appointment, I found 'stillborn' stickers which could be placed on the front of my maternity notes. This would not be the first time this question came up, and from that day forward, I continued to say that I have two daughters, because it is true.

At nineteen weeks she weighed in at ten ounces. All her organs were visible and in good working order. We bought a home foetal doppler, so we could listen twice daily to her heartbeat, that is if we could find it. Already she loved to get my blood pumping by skipping through the umbilicus, playing hide-and-seek behind the placenta, leisurely lounging around in all kinds of awkward positions. On many occasions, we heard an empty silence; this was when my own heart needed reviving. During semi-good days, there was a drum roll, which was the pulsation sounds coming from the umbilical cord and placenta combined. The bottom line was, home dopplers are not reliable, and they can be confusing to the untrained ears. These two vital organs needed to stay alive and keep intact to give her life until she was born. Her real heartbeat sounded more like Black Beauty galloping along the golden beaches of Cornwall with peregrine falcons flying at speed beside her. At twenty-one weeks, as a precaution, I had a glucose blood test where they diagnosed me with gestational diabetes. The consultant suggested a low dose of metformin, alongside a specially designed diabetic diet of zero sugar, high protein, full fat, low carbs. This combination of foods was to be eaten as three-square meals a day, along with three snacks in between. This time my rounded tummy was full of healthy balanced food and a growing baby, I could not have been happier.

Our fifth house since we met in 2010 sat in a quiet street in Aylesbury; luckily, it was four minutes away from the maternity unit. We were cautious about creating any kind of nursery for her in the spare room; instead, we had a small flexible cot next to our bed. The design tipped downwards at the front for reflux and colic issues, the side panel had mesh surrounds so not to suffocate, and it unzipped for easy access in the night. We had no fancy wall stickers or hanging mobiles, or a clutter of soft toys. So not to suffocate her by using blankets, she would sleep in a grow-suit, that zipped up the front like a sleeping bag, with her arms exposed. No cuddly toys would surround the bare basic cot, in case of asphyxiation. The fear of cot death was already looming before she had drawn her first breath.

The only thing left to do was think of a name. I had been a big fan of a French art film. The poster lived with me in all my homes, her name was literally written on the wall, screaming at me since 2001. Before we worked this out, other names such as Echo, Angel, Martha, and Emily came to mind for the second time, as Brian suggested this name before Molly came along. One Sunday morning, as I lay in bed listening to *Radio 6 Music*, the soundtrack of this film came on '*Comptine d' Un Autre – Rhyme of Another*', when a sudden spasm of lousy leg cramps along with a top-up twinge of heartburn attacked at that moment. Rubbing the lower part of my right leg, I looked upwards at the poster encased within its heavy wooden frame with gilt finish. Her name called out from behind framed glass. "Brian, I know her name!" Brian had been plumping up more cushions under my aching legs.

"Her name will be Amélie, spelt like the French film with the accent above the first é, yes, Amélie Mear, that is it, it fits." "How do you spell that?" he asked. Brian could not see how to spell it, as the poster was written in Japanese, and he did not know how to create the accent above the é on his new modern *Motorola Moto G* smartphone, that baffled him anyway.

Earthland orbited another three hundred and sixty-five days; the 12th of February 2017 had come around yet again. My exhausted, pregnant body slid over into its fiftieth year in Gregorian age. Amélie was still going strong at twenty-one weeks, as once predicted on our wedding day; indeed, I was pregnant with one baby on my fiftieth birthday. After Molly died, I truly felt that there was nothing left to live for, and at the time, my sorry life had seemed well and truly over. I still felt, since being taken away from my birth family at age fifteen, that I had failed at all thing's family ever since. However, here we were, four years later, now both in our fifties, still married to each other with another daughter on the way. I could also say that no one would ever have predicted this, but they all did! Most days, I glowed like a ready-brek commercial, full of health and vitality, not too chunky, sporting delicate slim ankles for the first time in years thanks to acupuncture and sensible eating. Mentally, I felt stronger, which was the key to completing this next mission into motherhood.

March 2017, we decided to put on another Mearfest, this time in Newcastle. Since our first successful Mearfest event in London, Brian had been inundated with requests from bands from the North East. Many bands had read our story online and wanted to play for us in support. So, he thought he would put a show on in Newcastle. At twenty-five weeks, we had not announced the pregnancy on Facebook; only our closest friends where aware, for apparent reasons. With Molly's now-infamous backdrop and one hundred light blue t-shirts with her darker blue handprint on them, which was not very heavy metal at all, we took a chance in printing a new colour t-shirt and hand for every event we did.

Saturday afternoon I went for a walk into Newcastle City centre. Moving at a steady pace, I momentarily paused to rest on a railing. There was a small, green, Romany gypsy caravan nearby, it was static on the pavement. A beautiful young woman was beckoning me with her index finger. "I have a message for you," she said. I bet she did, I thought aloud as I climbed up to the top of some rickety wooden steps. Squeezing through the miniature arched doorway, I sat upon a three-legged, hand-carved stool in front of the smallest log burner I had ever seen.

"Please do not tell me I am going to have a baby; this, I think, is very obvious!" We both laughed as I balanced my central force of gravity on the child's stool. "Of course, you are pregnant, but it is a girl, and you should have had twins this time. Oh dear, one baby died shortly after conception. You should have had five babies in your life, four have died. The girl you are having should have been a boy. If she were a boy, then she would be a great footballer, watch her with balls, she will be drawn to them. Yes, not a natural conception, needles, oh, IVF." Jeez, she was excellent, but four babies I did not understand, did I lose another one somewhere? I was gripped.

"You lost twins in your twenties, a full-term baby in your forties and this current baby's twin." She was spot on. She spoke with a strong Romany gypsy accent. "Your baby will be cheeky, in a funny way, she will want to make you laugh. I do not see her being an entertainer as such, um, there are stages, with many people looking at her." This sounded to me more Mearfest-related. "Your daughter will make you proud whatever she does in life, she will study hard, be clever, and be a good learner. You, my dear, will bring her confidence, and help her to understand how to survive in this world. Her world will be greatly different from your world. This is your task ahead." To hear some stranger say all this, confirmed everything I had ever wished for my child.

"One word of warning, you must not travel this far away from home after this weekend. Do not go far from your hospital, because I think she will come early. Please rest, and try to sleep. Remember she is a fighter, she is a survivor, she is going to be born alive, then will live to be an incredible woman. It is written in the stars. And, a final thing, a message from someone called Ada, she says thank you for setting their spirits free. Does this make any sense to you?" Yes, it did, my memory came back from when I birthed Molly and went somewhere else. Gratefully, I bought all her lucky charms and bunches of heather. It was such a joy to hear these words. Mearfest in the North East was a success. Our second charity event in Molly's name had sold out, as did all the blue t-shirts. Making new lifetime friends, we donated all the proceeds to Down syndrome North East, in Molly's name. This proved that the combination of heavy metal music and stillbirth worked, turning loss into legacy.

TWENTY-TWO

THE BEGINNING.

After the thirtieth week, there were a couple of scary occasions when I could not feel Amélie moving. This time I did not hesitate to call the midwife or labour ward. My gestational diabetes rapidly escalated, so I needed a higher dose of combined metformin and insulin. One afternoon, I awoke from a deep sleep in excruciating pain, both hips felt wonky, and I was unable to move either leg. Getting up from the bed was impossible, I was becoming paralysed with fear at thirty-four weeks. Brian insisted we go to the hospital, even though this felt more like some skeletal issue rather than a maternity one. Brian struggled to lift me to my feet, my awkward size did not help, and the pain had worsened. Screaming, I was at a loss of what to do. An ambulance had been called, the nurse in control tried to triage that I was in early labour, but my waters had not broken, and the pain was nowhere near the baby.

The trip to the hospital took three minutes, in that time I must have sucked up an entire cylinder of Entonox. Both sacroiliac joints were giving me bilateral lower back pain. These joints had a vital part to play within the birthing process. The hormone relaxin is typically produced during the late stages of pregnancy, which causes the ligaments of the sacroiliac joint to loosen up, enabling a more extensive range of movement. Pregnancy can be the first time this joint will be mobile since childhood. With Molly, I suffered more with my ankle and lower legs, due to falling out of an ambulance and tearing my ligaments, so this was a new pain.

Once within the safety of the labour ward, it was confirmed that I was not in labour. The nurses worked hard to ameliorate the atmosphere of worry. I was given morphine to assist with the pain, and they advised it best to stay in the hospital for monitoring. During the next three days, my body wanted to sleep, but I had to keep everything moving, walking round and round the same maternity level, to keep my joints fluid. I got to know all the midwives, porters, kitchen, and cleaning staff. Oddly, this one experience gave my over-sensitive mental state a rest from worry. Not only did I enjoy much-needed bed rest, as the morphine eased the excruciating pain, but I could also sleep more deeply without the fear she would die, something I had not done in months. The foetal monitor gave accurate cardiac readings which were noted down on charts every other hour; Amélie's birthing notes had originally stated another vaginal birth, with no fancy pools or holistic gizmos.

Returning home, my lower back still spasmed, but I declined any more pain relief, so as not to affect Amélie. That is when the thought came to my mind to phone Vince, the psychic surgeon, to see if there was anything he could do. He told me to wait two days, during that time, he would perform remote healing on this area, and with my permission, he will ask spirit Doctor Charles to work on me. Permission granted! A day later, propped up in the armchair, my head then eyes became heavy and dizzy as I sunk into a fathomless sleep-kind of trance. Upon waking, I got to my feet with no problems, yawning then stretching every revived muscle before waddling, pain-free, up the stairs to the bathroom and back.

The 12th of June 2017 was to be her fortieth-week due date, which would be the twins of Gemini, the chameleon of the zodiac. This would have been perfect if she had not lost her twin so soon. Keeping my cool appearing to be a thick-skinned Triggerfish gliding around in a calm lagoon, underneath I was a wooden barrel stuffed full of Bohemian crystal being thrown over Niagara Falls. The doubts started to niggle, was Amélie moving enough, could I feel her at night when sleeping? She usually moved a lot in the evenings, but she had begun to slow down, thus from thirty-five weeks onwards sleep became an outdated pastime. I feared she would float away just like her big sister, and I would again be none the wiser, becoming the mother of two late daughters.

This was when I first called the midwife in a panic. "Claire, I am amazed you have not called me before. Normally when someone has gone through full-term stillbirth as you have, and I am sorry to add, at your age, they panic from week one right up to the end." Was she praising me or telling me off? Had I been irresponsible, should I have come in earlier for more checks? We could hear Red Rum overtaking Black Beauty galloping to the finish line, bets were placed, 50/1 each way. "She is in there and moving well, listen to that careering, there she is the little pickle, her head is down. This is excellent news." The midwife tried her best to reassure, but my last midwife had said these exact words two days before Molly died.

Returning to Brixton to see Claire D for the final acupuncture session before Amélie was to be born in just over four weeks' time, I felt like a milestone had been reached, but it was not over quite yet. Claire D's face beamed with pride and joy, for we had gotten to this stage of last trimester late-term pregnancy, with no serious medical hiccups. Excitement filled her Brixton treatment room. Until this last week, I had tried my damnedest and kept my cool throughout, all thanks to her calming energising wisdom, affirmations, and needles. Claire D did something called the leg three-mile points, also known as *The Point of 100 Diseases*, this is a necessary pre-birth session. The title is due to its ability to enable the fatigued mother to find that extra three miles to the finishing line. Legend has it that Chinese warriors wore leather sashes with heavy stones hanging from either side of their waistbands or belts, kneeling on one leg to rest while hiking across the vast countryside. When rising to their feet, a renewed strength grounded them due to the pressure of the stones pushing in on those correlating pressure points of the body. These same points nourished my blood; they made me feel extra warrior brave, while at the same time boosting a struggling immune system, tonifying my Chi energy.

Once our final session had ended, tears of gratitude topped up water levels in Brockwell Park Lido up the road. This special lady had brought me back from the absolute brink of complete despair; through her, I became the seven billion-dollar woman whose confidence had been restored after trauma. She did rebuild me, she had the teachings, she made me believe that I was brilliant, sturdy, fertile. She masterfully taught me the difference between feeling empty and feeling hungry. During each session, she executed a skilful peeling of outer ruggedness along with a meticulous picking away at ME-go which I had created to get by alone in life. Now I was not alone anymore. She plunged her needles into weakened sinkholes of flesh, gently puncturing blocked toxic problems, lancing them wide open, releasing all psychological and physiological conditioning. Finally enabling the free flow of stagnant blood, she weeded out the recurring aggravation, which during private times alone had become an ocular irritant. My primary burden was still my birth-family.

We discussed my father and his weaknesses as a man. During this time before delivery, I needed to clear away vast amounts of built-up resentment. The original 1982 vintage bottle of pent-up emotions, still had residual sediment floating around. It had been corked, and still fermenting angrily in my gut. Even though I had spoken to him after he had passed over, I needed to release the physical man I once knew, as his spirit had returned to being pure love. My living mother was a different challenge. I had on a few occasions sent her various forms of olive branches, this was not effective as she continued to ignore my pleas for peace. During this time, I learnt something new about the beauty of IVF. When my Grandma Anna was pregnant with Rita, my mother, her baby ovaries were busy creating me. I would have absorbed Rita's and Anna's worries and traumatic life changes. When Rita was pregnant with me, my womb was busy designing my own batch of eggs, this meant Molly would have absorbed Rita's and my early teenage traumas. We were all absorbing each other's stories. Unlike Molly, Amélie was never in there, she was initially formed from the uterus of a Greek Goddess donor. I prayed she could not inherit my complicated strands of abandonment issues, going back to Grandma Anna, maybe further, from my just carrying her to full-term.

All babies are born virtuous; it is we, the grown-ups with our positive or negative talk which enhances or corrupts them. I did not want to pass any of this on to her, especially after she was born. Walking through Brixton that extra three miles, barefoot through a field of Chinese needles, helped me in my quest to one day end this painful, generational cycle of neglect for myself and my child to be. I knew it would be worth it in the end.

I wanted more than anything to prove to myself, and both parents, dead or alive, that anyone can turn the negative cycles of abuse and neglect around. I can only do this once she is here, and as she grows up. The rest of this utopian dream was now out of my hands and left up to science and the Gods.

On the thirty-sixth week, there had been little to no movement for most of the day. That instinctual feeling of doom resurfaced. We called the labour ward, luckily, I was on first name terms with them. Amélie's heart rate was indeed much slower than usual; the midwife decided to keep the monitor on for a good two hours; her heart rate did not change. The diabetic consultant explained that because of the complications of Molly's delivery, especially with the shoulder dystocia, they now preferred to perform an elective C-section on Monday the 22nd of May 2017, which would be on the thirty-seventh week exactly. This was considered full term. The number 22! I needed to come into the labour ward daily for monitoring until then. Going home each day from the labour ward was not easy; we were both consumed by images of being told the following morning that our baby was dead, as she could slip away at any time just like her big sister did, while I selfishly slept. I was trying my best to be mindful, tranquil, and watchful. Every second spent at home, I had the foetal doppler glued to my tummy. We made it to Friday the 19th of May, Amélie was thirty-six weeks and five days old, but it was still too early to pull her out. Since the trauma of Molly was ever-present as we began to glide down similar timelines; they finally decided to keep me in the hospital.

Monday the 22nd of May 2017, my baby's heartbeat was still very slow but steady. Brian stood by my side, refreshed from his weekend of uninterrupted sleep. The atmosphere in the theatre was not one of anticipated excitement and jubilation. The staff had all been briefed about what had happened to Molly. Sitting statue-still, in my somewhat undersized hospital gown that just about wrapped around my expectant body, clutching hold of a white pillow for dear life, I felt oddly serene as they plunged the epidural needle deep into my spine. Once the anaesthetic had taken hold, the numbness spread like dye in water. Lying flat on the theatre bed, the screen dividing us had been made from the bottom part of my ill-fitting hospital gown, which looped up on to metal rods.

I laid there, unable to feel anything but apprehension, staring at the clock on the wall. The minute hand slowed right down when at 16.00 GMT exact. The Sun had just ingressed from Taurus the day before; transiting one degree and 42 minutes into Gemini, when Amélie emerged. This little life had many studies to come, with her brand-new brilliant mind, she needed to communicate her clear visions to the world. This unique birth time gave her a bit of Jupiter, the planet of expansion. This influence will give Amélie much faith, to go beyond the point where most people wish to stay satisfied, just like her mummy. Listening intently, I had not heard her cry yet. Daddy Mear glided over to the station where the chief paediatrician checked our brand-new baby girl's entire body. I could not see what was going on, and still had not heard her cry, just a lot of rushing around in hushed silence. It was like a morgue during a pandemic.

My mind raced thinking the worst; then suddenly, everyone started talking at once, saying aloud how beautiful she is, not was! Amongst all this kerfuffle I heard her make a small cry. My God, that was my baby, alive with working lungs. My patience was running out. I could not wait for a second longer to see her for myself. Who had we made? As of four long minutes ago, I had become not just any old mother, but Mamma-Mear. The surgeons left a skipping rope length of umbilical cord for Brian to cut; he savoured the moment of finally being able to be the proudest father. *'Then I saw her face, not a trace of doubt was there in my mind. I was in love, I could never leave her, even if I tried.'*

Within a heartbeat, unconditional, enamoured devotion pumped new life around my anaesthetised body for this little creature; she was perfection, weighing 6 lbs and 6 oz. Her big cupid lips were ready to kiss. The gestational diabetic diet had worked. Both her tiny fists were curled up tight in a ball; there was not a chance of creating ink prints of either of them. Everyone in the room wore triumph upon their jubilant faces, fist-pumping the air with a couple of gloved high fives. Her placenta snuggly fitting within a metal bowl, which was considerably different from Molly's, that was dark red and in many pieces. Amélie's placenta was vibrant, bright red in colour, but most importantly, it was completely intact.

In the alternative UK charts that day, the number one song was, *'Believer'* by Imagine Dragons! From the heart of Athens to the spiritual cradle of Aylesbury, Brian and I had pushed believing and miracles to their absolute limits, and we never gave up hope in securing our dream. Aged fifty years, three months, ten days, twelve hours, and twenty-five minutes, I had become a mother for the second time. Our journey together was a full-on miracle. Amélie was our diamond in the coal, and now her special birth song, *'Believer,'* would be her new life mantra, just like mine was for me. My soul, my heart, my dedication, all came from faith.

"Clear the set, cut the lights that's a wrap folks, good job everybody!"

USEFUL CONTACTS

Mearfest Facebook:
www.facebook.com/mearfest4

Mearfest Website:
www.mearfest.org

The Willows Support Group (Berkshire):
www.willowssupportgroup.co.uk

SANDS (Stillbirth And Neonatal Death):
www.sands.org.uk

DSNE (Down Syndrome North East)
www.dsne.org.uk

Claire DaBreo:
www.thelondonacupuncturist.co.uk

Vincent Fuller
www.vincentfuller.co.uk

Serum IVF Clinic Athens:
www.ivfserum.com

If you have enjoyed this book, please share, and discuss with friends and family. Leave a review on Amazon, or on my social media and website, listed in contacts.

Thank you for taking the time to read my story.